TOPICS IN APPLIED ECONOMI

KENNETH F. WALLIS

# Topics in Applied Econometrics

Second Edition, Revised

University of Minnesota Press · Minneapolis

© Kenneth F. Wallis 1979
First edition published 1973
Second edition published 1980
in the United States of America
by the University of Minnesota Press,
Minneapolis, Minnesota 55414

**Library of Congress Cataloging in Publication Data**

Wallis, Kenneth Frank.
    Topics in applied econometrics.

    Bibliography: p.
    Includes index.
    1. Econometrics. I. Title.
HB141.W34 1980      330'.01'51      80-18456
ISBN 0-8166-1014-2
ISBN 0-8166-1017-7 (pbk.)

# CONTENTS

# PREFACE

This book discusses the formulation and empirical testing of economic hypotheses in four areas of application that are of considerable general interest. The emphasis throughout is on the interplay of economic theory and econometric methods, and there is no attempt to present a survey of the empirical work on each of the chosen topics. In general the studies selected for discussion have an interest beyond their particular numerical results, and contribute to the development of ideas and approaches that are capable of wider application. Some studies are presented rather fully without, it is hoped, getting too lost in their particular details. My aim is to inform and encourage those who approach empirical work in any field of economics, although statistical techniques that are specific to fields not discussed here are of course left on one side.

The first edition of this book originated in lectures given to students on a taught master's course in economics, and given the developments in the teaching of economics has subsequently been used in undergraduate courses in universities and polytechnics. For the present edition much of the material has been rewritten and reorganised, and recent developments and new empirical studies have been incorporated. Again I have not attempted to provide potted versions of the background material in mathematics, statistics and econometric methods that is required, for these often do the material a disservice, in my view, and there are many good texts available. The required mathematical background is well represented by Stephen Glaister's *Mathematical Methods for Economists*, and while my own *Introductory Econometrics* has often been used as a companion to the present volume, texts such as G. S. Maddala's *Econometrics* or J. Johnston's *Econometric Methods* provide a more extensive treatment of certain material, in particular estimation theory. There are expositions of technical points here and there throughout the book, which I hope follow naturally from the problems being discussed. My allocation of such items into those to be expounded herein and those to be referenced elsewhere may not be to every reader's taste, but reflects the organisation of courses in which I have been involved over the years.

Many teachers and students have made comments, criticisms and suggestions about this material, for which I am grateful, and I hope that this flow will continue. I am also grateful for the assistance of Kerrie Beale in preparing the final manuscript.

# I

# THE CONSUMPTION FUNCTION

## INTRODUCTION

The consumption function, describing the relation between consumption and income, plays a central role in Keynesian models of national income determination, and the question of what factors affect this relationship at the level of the individual household is of importance in many microeconomic problems. The concept of a consumption function originated in Keynes' *General Theory*, and subsequently has been the subject of considerable empirical study, probably to a greater extent than any other relation in economics. In this chapter we retrace the steps taken in developing and testing consumption theories, describing the interactions between theory and empirical evidence. Our discussion of the permanent income hypothesis includes consideration of a study which uses some theoretical results about instrumental variable estimators in the course of testing the theory. We conclude with some recent studies that were partly motivated by the failure of existing models to reflect the behaviour of consumption and saving in the early 1970's. We focus on the division of income into consumption and saving and leave aside questions of the allocation of consumption into individual expenditure categories, this latter topic (usually termed consumer demand analysis) being of book length in itself.

We start with Keynes' "fundamental psychological law" (*General Theory*, Chapter 8) that consumption increases as income increases, but not by as much as the increase in income. In the notation which has become standard for this model we denote consumption by $C$ and income by $Y$ and write the consumption function as

$$C = f(Y), \text{ with } 0 < \frac{dC}{dY} < 1.$$

Keynes further expected the proportion of income consumed to decrease as income increases, i.e. $d(C/Y)/dY < 0$, implying an income elasticity of consumption less than one, and from this follows the argument that redistribution of income in favour of the poor will raise aggregate demand. Further points are that changes in the money value of wealth cause short-period changes in the propensity to consume, and that the short-run marginal propensity to consume (m.p.c.) is less than the long-run m.p.c. This latter point follows from the argument that one's standard of living is inflexible in the short run, discrepancies between actual income and expenditure on this habitual standard going straight into savings, for habits require time to adapt to changed circumstances. These elements and others of Keynes' original specification have been used in empirical econometric work, as we shall see.

Both time series and cross-section data are relevant to an investigation of the exact form of the consumption function. Time series data from the national income accounts permit the determination of a relation explaining variations in aggregate consumers' expenditure, which might then become an element of a multi-equation model useful for macroeconomic forecasting and the evaluation of economic policies. Cross-section analysis, based on data collected from sample surveys of households, is often concerned with the role of other factors additional to income, such as age and household composition, occupation, and so forth. For both types of data the simplest formulation of the consumption function, useful at least as a first approximation, is the standard linear regression model

$$C = \alpha + \beta Y + u,$$

where $u$ is a random disturbance term. Here $C/Y$, the share of consumption in income or average propensity to consume (a.p.c.), decreases as income rises provided that $\alpha > 0$. The m.p.c. $\beta$ is assumed to satisfy $0<\beta<1$, but if this formulation is estimated from time series data there is no distinction between the short-run and the long-run m.p.c. Also with this linearisation the redistribution argument is no longer appropriate.

The original rationalisation suggests that the appropriate income variable to use in empirical work is personal disposable income, for it is constructed in terms of an individual determining the scale of consumption having net income in mind. Further, the absence of money illusion can be incorporated in this simple linear relation. The saving-consumption decision is assumed independent of the aggregate price level, hence the variables of the consumption function should be entered in real rather than nominal terms. Of course with cross-section data it can be reasonably assumed that prices do not vary across the sample, but with aggregate time series data an important first step is to deflate the current values of observed variables by an appropriate price index, to ensure that the correct statistical specification is employed. Thus if the appropriate model is

$$C_t = \alpha + \beta Y_t + u_t,$$

where the variables $C_t$ and $Y_t$ are in real terms and the disturbance $u_t$ has constant variance $E(u_t^2) = \sigma_u^2$, then a simple regression estimated from nominal variables, in effect $(C_tP_t)$ and $(Y_tP_t)$ where $P_t$ is the price level, is a serious misspecification. The model gives the relation between the nominal variables as

$$(C_tP_t) = \alpha P_t + \beta(Y_tP_t) + u_tP_t$$

so estimation of the equation

$$(C_tP_t) = \alpha' + \beta'(Y_tP_t) + v_t$$

yields biased and inconsistent estimates of $\alpha$ and $\beta$. Similarly, aggregate variables may be expressed in *per capita* terms if the sample period exhibits considerable changes in population, for with the appropriate model expressed at the individual or household level the same argument applies if $P_t$ is interpreted as the number of such units.

## ESTIMATES OF THE SIMPLE LINEAR CONSUMPTION FUNCTION

What happened when the simple linear consumption function was estimated by regression methods? A typical result is that given by Davis (1952), using U.S. annual data, 1929-1940, in billions of dollars, deflated for price and population changes:

$$C_t = 11.45 + 0.78\ Y_t, R^2 = .986$$
$$(.02)$$

(standard errors in parentheses). With $R^2$, the square of the correlation coefficient, taking a value of 0.986 the relation obviously fits the data well. However, despite this, when the relation was used to predict consumption in the immediate post-war period large positive forecast errors resulted: the relation consistently underpredicted consumption for 1946-1950. Such a contradiction between the sample period and the forecast period casts doubts on the simple linear formulation. But perhaps the poor predictions result from the inappropriate use of ordinary least squares (OLS) regression methods.

The conventional context in which "simultaneous equations bias" is demonstrated in econometrics texts is precisely that of the simplest Keynesian model obtained when the above consumption function is supplemented by the identity

$$Y_t = C_t + I_t.$$

This divides income into two components of effective demand, and the second, investment, is _assumed_ to be autonomous or exogenous or, in particular, independent of the disturbance $u_t$. Thus we have a pair of equations that jointly determine $C_t$ and $Y_t$ in terms of $I_t$ and $u_t$, and the solution for $Y_t$ is given by the reduced form equation

$$Y_t = \frac{1}{1-\beta}\ (\alpha + I_t + u_t).$$

The coefficient $1/(1-\beta)$ is of course the investment multiplier but more importantly for our present purpose the equation describes the relation between $Y_t$ and $u_t$. The existence of this relation implies the breakdown of one of the conventional assumptions of least squares regression, namely the independence of regressors and disturbances. Given a sample of $n$ observations the OLS estimate of $\beta$ is calculated as

$$\hat{\beta} = \sum_{t=1}^{n} y_t c_t \Big/ \sum_{t=1}^{n} y_t^2,$$

where lower-case letters denote deviations from the respective sample means: $c_t = C_t - \overline{C}$, $y_t = Y_t - \overline{Y}$. The properties of this procedure are then studied by substituting for $c_t$ from the consumption function and considering the sampling error $\hat{\beta} - \beta$. The random nature of $y_t$ implies that we can evaluate this only as the number of observations $n$ tends to infinity. Specifically the probability limit of the sampling error is calculated from

$$\text{plim} \, (\hat{\beta} - \beta) = \text{plim} \, \frac{1}{n} \Sigma \, y_t u_t \Big/ \text{plim} \, \frac{1}{n} \Sigma \, y_t^2$$

and by using the reduced form equation we obtain

$$\text{plim} \, (\hat{\beta} - \beta) = \frac{\sigma_u^2}{1-\beta} \Bigg/ \frac{\sigma_u^2 + \sigma_I^2}{(1-\beta)^2} = \frac{(1-\beta)\sigma_u^2}{\sigma_u^2 + \sigma_I^2}$$

where $\sigma_I^2$ is the limit of the expression $\Sigma(I_t - \overline{I})^2 / n$. The right-hand side gives the inconsistency in the OLS estimator, and this is seen to be positive. This is a large-sample result, but it can be taken as an indication that in finite samples $\beta$ will tend to be overestimated. This problem can be avoided by using a consistent estimator, and since the consumption function here is just-identified, an instrumental variable estimator is appropriate (and is identical to the indirect least squares estimator). Thus it is necessary to compute $b = \Sigma I_t c_t / \Sigma I_t y_t$ as a consistent estimate of $\beta$. An example is provided by Haavelmo (1947), using U.S. annual deflated *per capita* data, 1922-1941. The simple OLS regression of consumers' expenditure on disposable income yields $\hat{\beta} = 0.732$, while the instrumental variable estimate is $b = 0.672$. Thus despite the relatively small number of observations, the positive inconsistency in the OLS estimate shows through.

But none of this resolves the post-war forecasting problem: predictions were too low, not too high. A correct estimating procedure would have produced a lower estimate of $\beta$ and so increased post-war forecasting errors. Hence it became necessary to look for further empirical observations on which tests could be conducted and, more fundamentally, to extend the theory beyond the simple linear relationship.

A second difficulty emerged from other empirical work: the consumption-income ratio proved to be constant over long periods, contradicting the declining share hypothesis. Kuznets (1942) was the first researcher to produce this result, having studied U.S. national income data over the period 1879-1938, during which time national income quadrupled. This appeared to contradict the simple linear specification with $\alpha > 0$. Goldsmith (1955) subsequently confirmed Kuznets' finding for the more relevant aggregate variable, personal income.

Three further empirical points may be noted. First, though long-run time series studies apparently rejected the hypothesis that the consumption-income ratio declines with rising income, nonetheless cross-section (family budget) studies consistently supported the hypothesis. Secondly, cross-section studies continually produced smaller $\hat{\beta}$s than time series studies. This leads to the suggestion that

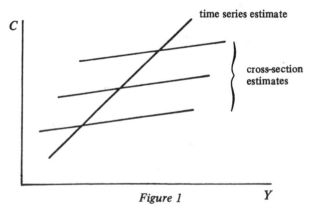

*Figure 1*

cross-section estimates could notionally be identified with the short term, relating to a moment in time. The flatter (lower $\hat{\beta}$) cross-section consumption functions might then move upwards over time, as illustrated in Figure 1. In this way the conflict between cross-section and time series estimates might be resolved in a way consistent with Keynesian theory. Lastly the aggregate consumption-income ratio fluctuated somewhat year by year despite the long-run tendency to constancy. Goldsmith detected cyclical variations in the ratio, which fell during periods of prosperity and rose during recessions, consumption respectively rising or falling proportionally less than income.

## THE RELATIVE INCOME HYPOTHESIS

Duesenberry (1949) attempted to explain these findings by a reformulation of consumption theory rather than a contribution to statistical methodology. His "relative income" hypothesis has consequences for both cross-section and time-series data. The cross-section effect derives from the hypothesis that a person's consumption behaviour is a function of his position in the income distribution or his "relative income", thus individual consumption behaviour is assumed to be interdependent, not independent. The time series effect depends on the idea that consumption behaviour is not readily reversible, and so people react differently to upward and downward income changes rather than having a simple consumption-income relationship equally applicable to income movements in either direction.

The cross-section formulation explains both the constant long-run share of consumption in rising income and the declining share observed in cross-section data. An individual household's consumption behaviour is assumed to depend upon its income percentile — a smaller proportion of income is consumed the higher the percentile position in the income distribution. If all incomes increase by the same proportion, relative incomes and hence consumption's share remain unchanged. Even if one household moves up to the next income group another must move down because income groups are defined in terms of percentiles. Hence aggregate consumption will remain unchanged. As a simple illustration of the relative income hypothesis, we might express the $i$th household's consumption-income ratio as a function of its relative income:

$$\frac{C_{it}}{Y_{it}} = \alpha_0 + \alpha_1 \frac{\overline{Y}_{.t}}{Y_{it}}$$

where $\overline{Y}_{.t}$ is the mean income of the group to which it belongs. Thus with $\alpha_1 > 0$ the share of consumption in income or a.p.c. declines as individual income increases. Equally, writing

$$C_{it} = \alpha_0 Y_{it} + \alpha_1 \overline{Y}_{.t}$$

shows that, at a point in time, the cross-section regression within a group has an m.p.c. equal to $\alpha_0$, and the function supports the declining share hypothesis, having a positive intercept term $\alpha_1 \overline{Y}_{.t}$. On aggregating over both individual households and groups, however, we see that the aggregate variables $C_t = \Sigma C_{it}$ and $Y_t = \Sigma Y_{it}$ satisfy the relation $C_t = (\alpha_0 + \alpha_1) Y_t$, thus the aggregate time series model not only yields an m.p.c. of $(\alpha_0 + \alpha_1)$, greater than the cross-section m.p.c., but also implies that the share of consumption in income remains constant as income increases over time.

Duesenberry explained the time series effect in terms of prior commitments, habit persistence, and so forth, concluding that "savings at a given level of income, when income is the highest ever attained . . . will be higher than savings at a similar income level reached in a decline from a still higher level" (p.89). Thus consumption will be higher than that predicted by the simple linear form when income falls. The consumption-income ratio depends on current income measured relative to the peak previous income, $Y_t^0$ say, and a linear approximation gives

$$C_t = \alpha + \beta_1 Y_t + \beta_2 Y_t^0$$

where $Y_t^0 = \max(Y_{t-j})$, $j \geq 1$. Then, if income is increasing over time, the peak previous income is always the last period's income, and the simple relationship between consumption and current income at time $t$ has an intercept term $(\alpha + \beta_2 Y_{t-1})$. This increases over time, and so the consumption-income relationship moves upwards, as illustrated in Figure 2. The slope of the solid lines is $\beta_1$, but in the second period the

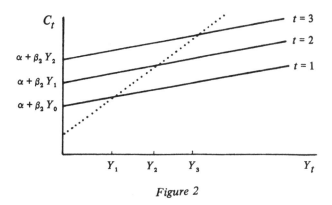

*Figure 2*

intercept is $\alpha + \beta_2 Y_1$, and so on. If income follows a linear trend, without cyclical fluctuations, $Y_t = Y_0 + \gamma t$ say, then observations lie along the dotted line in the chart, which has slope $\beta_1 + \beta_2$ and intercept term $\alpha - \beta_2 \gamma$: while not necessarily indicating a constant share, this does indicate rather less of a decline. However if income falls, $Y_t^0$ remains unchanged so the intercept does not shift and consumption falls back along one of the flatter "short-run" consumption functions. This is the so-called ratchet effect.

A precisely equivalent exposition can be given in terms of previous peak consumption $(C_t^0)$ rather than income:

$$C_t^0 = \max (C_{t-j}), \qquad j \geq 1$$

$$C_t = \alpha + \beta_1 Y_t + \beta_2 C_t^0.$$

As income, and thereby consumption, increases we can trace out a similar set of short-run functions giving a set of observations along a dotted line as in Figure 2. If income falls $C_t^0$ remains unchanged so consumption falls back along one of the flatter functions.

## DYNAMIC SPECIFICATIONS

Brown (1952) suggested that the influence of past habits is continuous in both directions rather than discrete and irreversible. He represented the dependence on past behaviour by including the lagged dependent variable rather than the previous peak of income or consumption among the regressors, so with aggregate time series data we have

$$C_t = \alpha + \beta_1 Y_t + \beta_2 C_{t-1}, \, 0 < \beta_2 < 1.$$

This modifies the Duesenberry pattern of behaviour to give continuous partial adjustment of consumption habits. In the second period of a decline the short-run function relating $C_t$ to $Y_t$ starts to drift back down the diagram again under the Brown hypothesis whereas, according to Duesenberry, consumption always moves back down the same short-run function which does not shift no matter how rapid the decline in income from the previous peak. This modification of the consumption function obeys the Keynesian requirement that the short-run marginal propensity to consume $\beta_1$ is less than the long-run m.p.c. $\beta_1 / (1 - \beta_2)$, which measures the increase in the equilibrium level of consumption in response to a unit increase in the level of income.

Brown set his consumption function in the context of a small macro-model, and estimated by appropriate simultaneous equations methods. For a two-equation model as used by Haavelmo, with $C_{t-1}$ added to the consumption function, the instrumental variable estimator remains appropriate as long as the error term is non-autocorrelated, which Brown found to be the case. Using annual Canadian data in constant dollars, 1926-1941 and 1946-1949, he reported a short-run m.p.c. of 0.40 and a long-run m.p.c. of 0.59. This seemed rather on the low side, when compared with Kuznets' estimate of the a.p.c. of 0.85-0.88.

Estimates of a similar function, among others, are reported by Evans (1969, §3.3), using annual U.S. data in constant dollars for 1929-1962 (excluding the American war years 1942-1946):

$$C_t = 0.280 \, Y_t + 0.676 \, C_{t-1}.$$
$$(.041) \qquad (.052)$$

The constant term is suppressed to give a constant a.p.c., in line with the results of Kuznets and Goldsmith. The dependent variable $C_t$ is consumption of non-durables and services: the reasons for excluding durables are discussed below. The estimated m.p.c.'s are short-run: 0.28 and long-run: 0.86, the latter being close to the a.p.c. for non-durables and services of 0.80.

Note that Evans, following Ball and Drake (1964), calculates long-run m.p.c.'s including an "allowance for growth". The argument for doing so is that the relation between the equilibrium values of consumption and income is calculated more realistically if the equilibrium is a growth path rather than a static position. In the context of the simple model

$$C_t = \beta_1 Y_t + \beta_2 C_{t-1}$$

$$Y_t = C_t + I_t$$

the nature of the steady-state growth path is determined by the behaviour over time of $I_t$. If $I_t$ has a constant value $I_0$, then the static equilibrium values $C^e$ and $Y^e$ are given by the solution of the static model

$$C^e = \beta_1 Y^e + \beta_2 C^e$$

$$Y^e = C^e + I_0$$

and the long-run m.p.c., measuring the relation between $C^e$ and $Y^e$, equal to the a.p.c. in this model, is given as $\beta_1/(1 - \beta_2)$. If $I_t$ grows exponentially, $I_t = (1 + g)^t I_0$, $g > 0$, then the equilibrium values of consumption and income exhibit the same behaviour: $C_t^e = (1 + g)^t C_0^e$ and $Y_t^e = (1 + g)^t Y_0^e$ where $C_0^e = aI_0$ and $Y_0^e = (1 + a)I_0$ with $a = (1+g)\beta_1/((1+g)(1-\beta_1)-\beta_2)$. The long-run m.p.c. is then given as $a/(1 + a)$, or equivalently by substituting $C_t/(1 + g)$ for $C_{t-1}$ in the dynamic consumption function, and either way we obtain a long-run m.p.c. of

$$\frac{\beta_1}{1 - \beta_2/(1 + g)} = \frac{(1 + g)\beta_1}{1 + g - \beta_2}.$$

Thus, compared with the static case in which $g = 0$, the long-run m.p.c. is diminished by the "autonomous" growth, but in practice few dramatic changes result given the usual order of magnitude of $g$. Evans takes $g = 0.02$, corresponding to 2% growth per annum, whereupon the long-run m.p.c. is estimated from the above results as 0.83, compared with 0.86 when $g = 0$. Note that the solution to the final equation for $C_t$ is, in general,

$$C_t - C_t^e = \left(\frac{\beta_2}{1-\beta_1}\right)^t (C_0 - C_0^e),$$

so that the question of stability, that is, of convergence to the steady-state growth path from an initial disequilibrium position, is assessed in the usual way: the stability condition for this model is $|\beta_2/(1 - \beta_1)| < 1$.

More recent estimates of a dynamic consumption-income relationship are provided for the U.K. by Davidson *et al.* (1978), using quarterly data for 1958I-1970IV. Seasonally unadjusted deflated data are employed, and after considerable investigation the following specification is selected:

$$\Delta_4 \log C_t = 0.49 \, \Delta_4 \log Y_t - 0.17 \, \Delta_1\Delta_4 \log Y_t - 0.06 \log (C/Y)_{t-4}$$
$$\phantom{\Delta_4 \log C_t =} (0.04) \phantom{\Delta_4 \log Y_t} (0.05) \phantom{\Delta_1\Delta_4 \log Y} (0.01)$$

$$+ \, 0.01 \, \Delta_4 D_t.$$
$$\phantom{+} (0.004)$$

The differencing operators are defined as $\Delta_1 X_t = X_t - X_{t-1}$ and $\Delta_4 X_t = X_t - X_{t-4}$, the latter appearing to remove seasonality satisfactorily. The dummy variable $D_t$ is designed to capture the switching of expenditure between the second and first quarters of 1968, which resulted from advance notice of purchase tax increases. The relationship is interpreted as a "feedback" model in which "consumers plan to spend in each quarter of a year the same as they spent in that quarter of the previous year ($\log C_t = \log C_{t-4}$) modified by a proportion of their annual change in income ($+0.49\Delta_4 \log Y_t$), and by whether that change is itself increasing or decreasing

$(-0.17\ \Delta_1\Delta_4\ \log Y_t)$; these together determine a 'short-run' consumption decision which is altered by $-0.06 \log (C/Y)_{t-4}$, the feedback from the previous $C/Y$ ratio ensuring coherence with the long-run 'target' outcome $C_t = kY_t$," (p.684). On a steady-state growth path with constant annual real growth rate $g$, i.e. $C_t^e = (1 + g)C_{t-4}^e$ or $\Delta_4 \log C_t^e = g$ using the approximation $\log (1 + g) = g$ for small $g$, the relation yields the solution

$$\log C^e - \log Y^e = (-0.51/0.06)g$$

or $C^e = kY^e$ where $k = \exp(-8.5\ g)$. Thus the long-run income *elasticity* of expenditure is unity, and with $g = 0.02$, as was approximately true during the sample period, we obtain a long-run m.p.c. (equal to the a.p.c. in this model) of $k = 0.84$.

## THE PERMANENT INCOME HYPOTHESIS

The next major contribution to the development of the consumption function that we discuss is the permanent income hypothesis of Friedman (1957). As we shall see, its statistical implications provide an explanation for some of the empirical phenomena noted above.

The basic idea is that the consumer disregards fortuitous variations in income when drawing up consumption plans; only expected, "normal", or permanent income $Y_P$ is considered. This is defined as the amount that the consumer unit believes it can consume whilst maintaining its wealth intact. The discrepancy between observed current or measured income $Y$ and $Y_P$ is termed transitory income $Y_T$, thus $Y = Y_P + Y_T$. Consumption is likewise divided into permanent or planned and transitory components $C_P$ and $C_T$ respectively, and $C = C_P + C_T$. An allowance for services derived from stocks of durable goods is included in the definition of $C_P$, and purchases of durables are treated as investment.

In drawing up its consumption plans the consumer unit only has in mind its permanent income, and the ratio of permanent consumption to permanent income is independent of $Y_P$:

$$C_P = kY_P.$$

Thus Friedman's consumption function has no intercept term, with the consequence that the long-run m.p.c. ($k$) is equal to the a.p.c. in accordance with the Kuznets-Goldsmith type of evidence. The ratio $k$ may in turn depend upon various factors such as the individual's discount rate, his portfolio of assets, tastes, and demographic factors (age, household composition, etc.). While Keynes had suggested that the income elasticity of consumption will be less than one, that is,

$$0 < \frac{d \log C}{d \log Y} = \frac{Y}{C}\frac{dC}{dY} < 1,$$

in this model the elasticity of (permanent) consumption with respect to (permanent) income is one.

As it stands the hypothesis has little substantive content, for we simply have two definitions introducing unobservable components together with the postulated relation between the permanent components. The specification of the statistical properties of the transitory components adds substance to the hypothesis and leads to the possibility of its testing. The remaining assumptions are

(i) the transitory components have zero means:

$$E(Y_T) = E(C_T) = 0,$$

(ii) the covariances between the permanent components and the corresponding transitory components are zero:

$$\mathrm{cov}(C_P, C_T) = \mathrm{cov}(Y_P, Y_T) = 0,$$

(iii) the transitory components of income and consumption are uncorrelated with one another:

$$\mathrm{cov}(C_T, Y_T) = 0.$$

This last is the strongest assumption for $E(C_T Y_T) = 0$ implies that a windfall gain will be saved (in the Friedman sense of not being spent on non-durable goods and services): a positive value of $Y_T$ will not lead to expenditure over and above the consumption plan.

This specification of the consumption function corresponds to that of the classical statistical "errors in variables" model. The true variables obey an exact functional relationship, but they are observed with error. The result is that least squares estimation of $C_P = kY_P$ using the observed variables $C$ and $Y$ gives an inconsistent estimate of $k$. This situation provides yet another example of bias in least squares estimates of consumption functions, and a further possible explanation of the least squares results. Observed consumption $C$ is given by

$$C = C_P + C_T = kY_P + C_T$$

and is thus related to observed income as follows

$$C = kY + (C_T - kY_T).$$

This gives a linear relationship between the observed variables, together with an error term $(C_T - kY_T)$ which is itself a function of the two transitory components. In particular $Y_T$ is a component of the explanatory variable and also appears in the error term, so we expect to find a non-zero covariance between $Y$ and $(C_T - kY_T)$, since there is no covariance between $C_T$ and $Y$ to set against the covariance between $Y_T$ and $Y$. Thus the requirement in the classical linear regression model of independence of regressors and disturbances breaks down, and the OLS estimator is inconsistent. The breakdown of this assumption due to the endogeneity of the regressor produced the simultaneous equation bias discussed above, but the circumstances of the present breakdown are rather different. Let us now examine the nature of the inconsistency.

Given data $\{C_i, Y_i\}$ $i = 1, \ldots, n$ for a sample of time periods or households, consider the usual least squares regression coefficient

$$\hat{\beta} = \frac{\Sigma c_i y_i}{\Sigma y_i^2}$$

where lower-case letters again denote deviations from sample means. To consider the properties of this method we substitute for $c_i$ from the model and utilize the statistical assumptions. The first step gives

$$\hat{\beta} = \frac{\Sigma(ky_{Pi} + c_{Ti})(y_{Pi} + y_{Ti})}{\Sigma y_i^2}$$

$$= \frac{\frac{1}{n}\Sigma(ky_{Pi}^2 + ky_{Pi}y_{Ti} + c_{Ti}y_{Pi} + c_{Ti}y_{Ti})}{\frac{1}{n}\Sigma y_i^2}.$$

Since the random variable $y$ appears in both numerator and denominator again we must resort to large-sample arguments and evaluate the probability limits of the numerator and denominator. By virtue of assumptions (ii) and (iii) above the covariances represented by the last three terms in the numerator all have zero probability limits, this result being obtained for the next-to-last term after the substitution of $c_{Pi}/k$ for $y_{Pi}$ and the application of assumption (ii). The remaining terms give the variances of permanent income and observed income, thus the probability limit of the least squares coefficient in the simple consumption-income regression is given, under the permanent income hypothesis, as

$$\text{plim } \hat{\beta} = k \frac{\text{var}(Y_P)}{\text{var }(Y)}.$$

Since $\text{var}(Y) = \text{var}(Y_P) + \text{var}(Y_T)$, we have

$$\text{plim } \hat{\beta} < k.$$

So the m.p.c. tends to be underestimated by the simple linear regression coefficient, the more so the greater the relative variance of transitory income.

Likewise an estimate of the income elasticity of consumption based on the least squares regression coefficient tends to be below the unit elasticity of the permanent income model. The estimate calculated at the sample means of the variables is

$$\hat{\eta} = \hat{\beta}\frac{\overline{Y}}{\overline{C}},$$

namely the least squares coefficient divided by the average propensity to consume. First note that the a.p.c. is a consistent estimator of $k$, since

$$\text{plim}\,\frac{\overline{C}}{\overline{Y}} = \frac{\text{plim}\,\frac{1}{n}\Sigma C_i}{\text{plim}\,\frac{1}{n}\Sigma Y_i} = \frac{\text{plim}\,\frac{1}{n}\Sigma C_{Pi}}{\text{plim}\,\frac{1}{n}\Sigma Y_{Pi}} = \frac{\text{plim}\,\frac{1}{n}\Sigma k Y_{Pi}}{\text{plim}\,\frac{1}{n}\Sigma Y_{Pi}} = k.$$

(Of course the a.p.c. may not be a very efficient estimator of $k$, but consistency is all that concerns us at the moment.) So considering the elasticity estimate we have

$$\text{plim}\,\hat{\eta} = (\text{plim}\,\hat{\beta})/\text{plim}\,\frac{\overline{C}}{\overline{Y}} = k\frac{\text{var}(Y_P)}{\text{var}(Y)}\cdot\frac{1}{k} = \frac{\text{var}(Y_P)}{\text{var}(Y)} < 1.$$

Again this is a large-sample result, which is nevertheless taken to suggest that in practical situations estimates of the elasticity tend to lie below one, even when the permanent income hypothesis is true. Also the estimated elasticity falls as the contribution of permanent income to the variance of observed income decreases.

It might be asked whether the emphasis on the simple linear regression model including a constant term is misplaced, since Friedman's consumption function has no intercept. But the source of the downward bias is the errors-in-variables problem, and this is not avoided by running a regression through the origin, that is, by working with the coefficient

$$\tilde{\beta} = \frac{\Sigma C_i Y_i}{\Sigma Y_i^2}.$$

A similar argument to that given previously leads to the result

$$\text{plim } \bar{\beta} = k \frac{\text{var}(Y_P) + \mu^2}{\text{var}(Y) + \mu^2}$$

where $\mu$ is the mean of permanent income (and of measured income, since transitory income is assumed to have a zero mean). Thus the relationship between the two regression estimates is

$$\text{plim } \hat{\beta} < \text{plim } \bar{\beta} < k,$$

so that a regression through the origin still tends to produce an underestimate of $k$ though not by as much as a regression including an intercept.

So far we have said nothing about whether the data used in the exercise are from cross-section or time series samples: the results hold for both. With cross-section data, one would expect that the least squares estimate of the m.p.c. for a group whose income contains a relatively important transitory component would be smaller than that of other groups. Friedman examined farm families in this light – their observed incomes are more variable, with the transitory component contributing relatively more to the total variation. He therefore expected to find that their estimated income elasticity of consumption would be less than that of non-farm families, and the hypothesis was corroborated. Similarly cross-section elasticity estimates for different years show the lowest values for the war year 1944, when the transitory component was relatively important, as would be expected in an unsettled period.

Applying the preceding arguments to time series data, the hypothesis suggests that the m.p.c. estimated by simple regression will be lower for shorter data periods, when there is less secular change in income and so smaller variation in the permanent component, and Friedman found that this was the case. The hypothesis suggests no generalisation about the relation between time series and cross-section estimates, both depending on the income structure in the sample. Nevertheless it is not surprising that the above time series estimate for 1929-1940, a period of stagnation and sharp short-period movements, is rather lower not only than estimates for other periods but also than estimates obtained from budget studies.

In this way the permanent income model can be used to cast light on the simple linear regression findings, but there remains the problem of developing more appropriate estimation procedures, in particular of consistently estimating $k$, and to this we now turn.

### AGGREGATE TIME SERIES ESTIMATES UNDER THE PERMANENT INCOME HYPOTHESIS

It is desired to estimate directly the permanent income consumption function $C_P = kY_P$ in a time series context, and the question of appropriate data immediately arises. First, for the dependent variable, the conventional use of the published series on consumers' expenditure on non-durables and services has both statistical and economic justification. Considering the statistical errors-in-variables model, note that the "error" $C_T$ in the dependent variable is not the source of the inconsistency in the estimate of $k$ described above, indeed being assumed independent of the explanatory variable $Y_P$ it plays the role of the usual regression disturbance term. The use of observed variables that differ from the true theoretical variables by a random error causes difficulties when such variables are regressors, but not when such a variable is the dependent variable. In Friedman's economic model consumers' expenditure on durable goods is treated as investment, and consumption should include the value of services derived from the stock of durable goods. This last objective cannot be achieved using conventional macroeconomic aggregates, and the error is transferred across to the disturbance term as already noted. But there has been general acceptance of the argument for excluding durables, and when separate models of expenditure on durables and non-durables have been estimated, they have typically exhibited responses to income that differ in respect of both long-run multipliers and short-run dynamic patterns.

If permanent income is unobservable, what variable should be entered on the right-hand side of the equation? To represent the relation between what people consider to be permanent income and past values of measured income Friedman employed "expected normal" income, constructed according to the adaptive expectations hypothesis introduced in Cagan's (1958) work on hyperinflation. In continuous time the hypothesis has the following differential equation formulation

$$\frac{\mathrm{d}Y_{Pt}}{\mathrm{d}t} = \theta(Y_t - Y_{Pt}),$$

whereby permanent income changes in response to discrepancies between observed and permanent income. On integrating we obtain

$$Y_{Pt} = \theta \int_0^\infty e^{-\theta\tau}\, Y_{t-\tau}\, \mathrm{d}\tau,$$

giving an exponentially weighted moving average type of expression. This can be extended to incorporate the effect of a correctly anticipated normal growth rate of income. Friedman then utilised a discrete-time approximation to this expression, having only annual data available. Thus permanent income was estimated as a moving average of current and past income with geometrically declining weights, and as a further approximation this distributed lag function was truncated after the first seventeen terms:

$$\hat{Y}_{Pt} = (1 - \gamma) \sum_{j=0}^{16} \gamma^j\, Y_{t-j}.$$

For estimation purposes Friedman constructed a number of $\hat{Y}_{Pt}$ series, using a different value of $\gamma$ in each case, ran the consumption function regression for each series (using data in real, *per capita* terms), and chose that value of $\gamma$ (and associated regression coefficients) which produced the highest $R^2$. The best estimate of the linear relation between $C_t$ and $\hat{Y}_{Pt}$ produced a *t*-ratio for the intercept term of 0.24, which was accepted as support for the hypothesis of a proportional relationship $C_{Pt} = kY_{Pt}$. The estimate of $k$ was 0.88, which was quite close to the observed average propensity to consume (which provides a consistent estimate of $k$). The estimate of the distributed lag coefficient implied an average lag of 2½ years.

Subsequently it was recognised that it is not necessary to truncate the above distributed lag function, but that the infinite geometrically-weighted distributed lag can be eliminated by the use of the transformation introduced by Koyck (1954). Thus with the model

$$C_t = kY_{Pt}, \quad Y_{Pt} = (1 - \gamma) \sum_{j=0}^{\infty} \gamma^j Y_{t-j}$$

on subtracting $\gamma$ times the lagged value of each side of the equation and rearranging, we obtain

$$C_t = \gamma C_{t-1} + k(1 - \gamma)Y_t .$$

In consequence "permanent income" ideas have often been used to justify the presence of the lagged dependent variable in a regression equation, even though the full permanent income theory might not be adopted by the investigator. If the suppression of the constant term is overlooked, then the regression equation is of the same form as that used by Brown, and the permanent income/adaptive expectations and partial adjustment hypotheses are often treated as observationally indistinguishable. Both hypotheses are somewhat *ad hoc*, since they are not based on any description of economic behaviour, but let us consider the extent to which they are equivalent by including an additional regressor variable and adding a disturbance term to the equation determining the observable dependent variable.

The partial adjustment model can be written

$$C_t^* = \alpha + \beta_1 Y_t + \beta_2 X_t ,$$

$$C_t - C_{t-1} = (1 - \gamma)(C_t^* - C_{t-1}) + u_t .$$

The first equation describes the determination of the unobservable "target", "desired" or "equilibrium" consumption in terms of explanatory variables $Y$ and $X$, and the second states that in any single period, the change in observed consumption is only a part of that required to achieve the desired level $(0 < \gamma < 1)$, due to inertia, lags in adjustment, and so forth. On substituting and rearranging, we obtain

$$C_t = \alpha(1 - \gamma) + \gamma C_{t-1} + \beta_1(1 - \gamma)Y_t + \beta_2(1 - \gamma)X_t + u_t.$$

The adaptive expectations/permanent income model is

$$C_t = \alpha + \beta_1 Y_t^* + \beta_2 X_t + u_t$$
$$Y_t^* = (1 - \gamma) \sum_{j=0}^{\infty} \gamma^j Y_{t-j}$$

or $\quad Y_t^* = (1 - \gamma)Y_t + \gamma Y_{t-1}^*.$

Substituting for $Y_t^*$ in the first equation and applying the Koyck transformation gives

$$C_t = \alpha(1 - \gamma) + \gamma C_{t-1} + \beta_1(1 - \gamma)Y_t + \beta_2 X_t - \beta_2 \gamma X_{t-1} + v_t$$

where $v_t = u_t - \gamma u_{t-1}$. First ignoring the disturbance term we see that the regression equations are identical if $\beta_2 = 0$, i.e. if the variable $X$ does not appear, but otherwise the adaptive expectations regression equation includes the lagged value of this variable, whereas the partial adjustment model does not. Moreover the coefficient of $X_{t-1}$ depends on the coefficients of $C_{t-1}$ and $X_t$, and this restriction might be imposed and/or tested in estimation. Secondly the transformation changes the autocorrelation pattern of the disturbance in the second equation: if the original disturbance $u_t$ is free of autocorrelation, then the disturbance $v_t$ is not. Thus, with $0 < \gamma < 1$, the error in the adaptive expectations regression equation might be expected to exhibit negative autocorrelation, and although this error term is a moving average of the original error, many investigators have used the first-order auto-regressive scheme $v_t = \rho v_{t-1} + \epsilon_t$ as an approximation. Below we consider an example of estimation subject to a moving average error specification, incorporating the restrictions that result from the appearance of the parameter $\gamma$ in so many places in the equation. Before that we consider further developments in testing the permanent income hypothesis, based on cross-section data.

## TESTS BASED ON A RE-INTERVIEW SAVINGS SURVEY

Liviatan (1963) has cross-section data on urban families in Israel, each of which was interviewed in two consecutive years. In principle time series observations on a cross-section of households (or "panel" data) offer the prospect of measuring the variability of income of individual households which, according to the preceding analysis, affects the estimates of the m.p.c. However with only two years' data a direct attack on this problem is not possible, nevertheless Liviatan's study provides an interesting illustration of the interplay between theoretical considerations and empirical evidence.

First we consider a test using estimates calculated from the *changes* in income and consumption between the two years. Given data $\{C_{it}, Y_{it}\}, i=1,\ldots,n, t=1,2$, the changes are calculated as $\Delta C_i = C_{i2} - C_{i1}$, $\Delta Y_i = Y_{i2} - Y_{i1}$, and the least squares coefficient obtained from these data is denoted

$$\hat{\beta}_\Delta = \frac{\Sigma \Delta c_i \Delta y_i}{\Sigma (\Delta y_i)^2} .$$

In the context of the simple Keynesian consumption function $C = \alpha + \beta Y + u$ the coefficient $\hat{\beta}_\Delta$ is a consistent estimator of $\beta$, and so one would not expect to find a systematic difference between this coefficient and the usual regression coefficient $\hat{\beta}$. The fact that a systematic difference between the two coefficients would be expected under the permanent income hypothesis provides an opportunity of comparing the two formulations. Let us examine the source of this difference.

We already have the result that under the permanent income hypothesis

$$\text{plim } \hat{\beta} = k \frac{\text{var}(Y_P)}{\text{var}(Y)},$$

and by the same procedure we obtain

$$\text{plim } \hat{\beta}_\Delta = k \frac{\text{var}(\Delta Y_P)}{\text{var}(\Delta Y)}.$$

This last result requires a slight extension of assumptions (ii) and (iii) above so that zero covariances between the relevant components in any time period are assumed. The numerator can be expanded to give

$$\text{var}(Y_{P2} - Y_{P1}) = \text{var}(Y_{P1}) + \text{var}(Y_{P2}) - 2\,\text{cov}(Y_{P1}, Y_{P2})$$

$$= 2\big\{\text{var}(Y_p) - \text{cov}(Y_{P1}, Y_{P2})\big\}.$$

if it is assumed that the variances in the two years are equal. If it is further assumed that the transitory components of income in the two years are uncorrelated, the denominator can be written

$$\text{var}(Y_2 - Y_1) = 2\big\{\text{var}(Y_P) + \text{var}(Y_T) - \text{cov}(Y_{P1}, Y_{P2})\big\}.$$

Since the permanent components in the two years are positively correlated, indeed Friedman assumes that they will be highly correlated, we have the inequality

$$\text{plim } \hat{\beta}_\Delta = k \frac{\text{var}(Y_P) - \text{cov}(Y_{P1}, Y_{P2})}{\text{var}(Y_P) + \text{var}(Y_T) - \text{cov}(Y_{P1}, Y_{P2})}$$

$$< \text{plim } \hat{\beta} = k \frac{\text{var}(Y_P)}{\text{var}(Y_P) + \text{var}(Y_T)}$$

and so under the permanent income hypothesis we expect to find $\hat{\beta}_\Delta < \hat{\beta}$.

In Liviatan's results $\hat{\beta}_\Delta$ is smaller than $\hat{\beta}$, but not substantially so, which is rather unfavourable to the permanent income hypothesis. Unfortunately, to carry out this test of the hypothesis, additional assumptions have been made (that the correlation between successive values of the income components is high for $Y_P$ and zero for $Y_T$) and it is not clear in such a situation whether the basic hypothesis or the additional assumptions are at fault. A further possible explanation rests on the fact that the data are from a savings survey rather than an expenditure survey, so that any measurement error in income is automatically transmitted to the estimate of consumption. Suppose that observed income is equal to $(Y_P + Y_T + e)$, then estimated consumption, calculated as observed income less savings, is equal to $(C_P + C_T + e)$, and so has a measurement error equal to that in observed income. Such common errors would increase the covariance between the observed income and consumption series, the data apparently negating the assumption that $C_T$ and $Y_T$ are uncorrelated when it is in fact true. Consequently Liviatan turns to methods which attempt to eliminate the influence of errors in the observed variables.

The instrumental variable (IV) method can be used to provide a consistent estimator in the errors-in-variables model, just as in our previous example of correlation between regressor and disturbance which give rise to "simultaneous equations bias". Given an instrumental variable $Z$, the IV estimator of the m.p.c. is

$$b = \frac{\Sigma c_i z_i}{\Sigma y_i z_i}.$$

If $Z$ is correlated with $Y_P$ but is independent of $C_T$ and $Y_T$ then $b$ is a consistent estimate of $k$:

$$\text{plim } b = \frac{\text{plim} \frac{1}{n} \Sigma (k y_{Pi} + c_{Ti}) z_i}{\text{plim} \frac{1}{n} \Sigma (y_{Pi} + y_{Ti}) z_i} = \frac{\text{plim} \frac{1}{n} \Sigma k y_{Pi} z_i}{\text{plim} \frac{1}{n} \Sigma y_{Pi} z_i} = k.$$

If the least squares coefficient $\hat{\beta}$, which tends to underestimate $k$ under the permanent income hypothesis, is substantially below $b$, which does not, then we shall have corroborative evidence in favour of the hypothesis. But what variable in the model can be used as an appropriate instrument?

To calculate the coefficient $b$ from cross-section data for a single year Liviatan first suggests that income in the other year be used as the instrument. Doing this for each of the two years, and for each of two sub-groups of his sample (employees and self-employed), Liviatan finds two highly significant differences between $\hat{\beta}$ and $b$, which support the permanent income hypothesis, and two which do not. However even in the favourable cases the estimated income elasticity remains less than one.

The consistency of $b$ requires the instrumental variable to be independent of the error $(C_T - kY_T)$, so that in the present context the transitory components of income in the two years are required to be independent, in particular. However in some of his own work Friedman suggests that the consumer's horizon is more than two years, so that Liviatan's data may include sub-periods of the same planning period, leading to positive correlation between the two transitory components. Such a correlation produces another downward bias in $b$. Denoting the income for the year in question by $Y$ (or $y$, in mean deviation form) and the other year's income, used as an instrumental variable, by $Y^*$ ($y^*$), and retaining the assumption that the permanent component is independent of the transitory component in either year, the above equation gives

$$\text{plim } b = \frac{\text{plim} \frac{1}{n} \Sigma k y_{Pi}(y_{Pi}^* + y_{Ti}^*)}{\text{plim} \frac{1}{n} \Sigma (y_{Pi} + y_{Ti})(y_{Pi}^* + y_{Ti}^*)}$$

$$= k \frac{\text{plim} \frac{1}{n} \Sigma y_{Pi} y_{Pi}^*}{\text{plim} \frac{1}{n} \Sigma (y_{Pi} y_{Pi}^* + y_{Ti} y_{Ti}^*)}.$$

Thus positive correlation between $Y_T$ and $Y_T^*$ serves to increase the denominator, leading to plim $b < k$. This could provide an explanation for the two non-significant differences between $\hat{\beta}$ and $b$, and for the elasticity estimates below one.

Is there another instrumental variable to hand? The other year's consumption, $C^*$, will provide a consistent estimate again if the transitory components are uncorrelated. What if $C_T$ and $C_T^*$ are positively correlated? It turns out that in this case $b$ will tend to overestimate $k$:

$$b = \frac{\Sigma c_i c_i^*}{\Sigma y_i c_i^*} = \frac{\Sigma (ky_i + c_{Ti} - ky_{Ti})c_i^*}{\Sigma y_i c_i^*}$$

$$= k + \frac{\Sigma (c_{Ti} - ky_{Ti})(c_{Pi}^* + c_{Ti}^*)}{\Sigma y_i c_i^*}.$$

Under the usual assumptions about the transitory components and serial independence of $C_T$, plim $b = k$ as before. But if $\text{cov}(C_T, C_T^*) > 0$ then plim $b > k$. So a calculated $b$ still less than the a.p.c., that is an estimated elasticity still less than one, despite this upward bias, contradicts the permanent income hypothesis. Now if durables are included in consumption expenditures, there may be negative correlation between transitory components, as Friedman comments, for a positive discrepancy from planned purchases of durables this year might be associated with a negative discrepancy next year. Indeed Liviatan does obtain higher values of $b$ when durables are excluded. But even then, Liviatan finds that $b$ is less than the a.p.c., despite the upward bias, and so Friedman's model is contradicted by the data. In his reply, Friedman appraises the findings cautiously: "If these results should be confirmed for other bodies of data, they would constitute relevant and significant evidence that the elasticity of permanent components is less than unity".

### ESTIMATES BASED ON THE OXFORD SAVINGS SURVEY

The assumption that transitory income has no effect on current consumption is controversial, but has proved difficult to test given the unobservable nature of the income components. In the time series context, permanent income may be estimated as a distributed lag function of actual income, as we have seen, but in general such estimates do not satisfy the assumption of the permanent income hypothesis that permanent and transitory components of income are uncorrelated, and if a particular aspect of the theory is rejected in a test based on such data it is seldom clear whether the theory itself or the construction of the estimates of the unobservables is at fault. In the cross-section context, while Liviatan's data do not contain information on components of income, such information is contained in the 1953 Oxford Savings Survey, allowing Attfield (1976) to test the controversial assumption noted at the opening of this paragraph. The data not only contain information on sweepstake and football pool winnings, legacies and gifts, considered to be items of transitory income, but also provide details of factors determining human and non-human wealth, i.e. determinants of permanent income, such as age, occupation, family size, net worth and rateable value of the property occupied.

The model used by Attfield relaxes the assumption of zero correlation between $C_T$ and $Y_T$, and adds relations determining $Y_P$ and $Y_T$, as follows:

$$Y_i = Y_{Pi} + Y_{Ti}$$
$$C_i = C_{Pi} + C_{Ti}$$
$$C_{Pi} = k_1 Y_{Pi}$$
$$C_{Ti} = k_2 Y_{Ti} + u_{1i}$$
$$Y_{Pi} = w_i' \beta + u_{2i}$$
$$Y_{Ti} = \alpha Z_i + u_{3i}$$

Thus the m.p.c.s out of permanent and transitory income are respectively denoted $k_1$ and $k_2$, and if $k_2 = 0$ the transitory components are uncorrelated. The vector $w_i$ is a $7 \times 1$ vector of determinants of permanent income, and $Z_i$ denotes unanticipated gambling gains, legacies and gifts, a potential element of transitory income. The random disturbances $u_{ji}$ are mutually uncorrelated, in accordance with the original stochastic specification. Given data on $n = 1306$ households, Attfield proceeds to estimate the parameters $k_1$, $k_2$, $\alpha$ and $\beta$ by a maximum likelihood procedure, which we can visualize by writing the relations between the observables implied by the model as

$$Y_i = \mathbf{w}_i' \beta + \alpha Z_i + v_{1i}$$
$$C_i = \mathbf{w}_i' \beta\, k_1 + k_2\, \alpha Z_i + v_{2i}$$

where

$$v_{1i} = u_{2i} + u_{3i} \text{ and } v_{2i} = u_{1i} + k_1 u_{2i} + k_2 u_{3i}.$$

These $2n$ relations can be collected together by defining a vector of observations on the dependent variables $\mathbf{y} = (Y_1, Y_2, \ldots, Y_n, C_1, C_2, \ldots, C_n)'$, a $2n \times 16$ matrix $\mathbf{X}$ whose $i$th row is $(\mathbf{w}_i', Z_i, 0, \ldots, 0)$ for $i = 1, \ldots, n$ and $(0, \ldots, 0, \mathbf{w}_{i-n}', Z_{i-n})$ for $i = n + 1, \ldots, 2n$, a vector of coefficients $\gamma' = (\beta', \alpha, k_1\beta', k_2\alpha)$, and a vector of disturbances $\mathbf{v} = (v_{11}, v_{12}, \ldots, v_{1n}, v_{21}, v_{22}, \ldots, v_{2n})'$, whereupon the above relations can be written

$$\mathbf{y} = \mathbf{X}\gamma + \mathbf{v}.$$

This is of the form of a standard regression model, except that the 16 elements of the coefficient vector are functions of only 10 parameters, and the error covariance matrix $E(\mathbf{vv}')$ is not of the simple $\sigma^2\mathbf{I}$ form, since $E(v_{1i}^2) = \sigma_1^2 \neq E(v_{2i}^2) = \sigma_2^2$ and $E(v_{1i}v_{2j}) = \sigma_{12}$ if $i=j$ due to the presence of structural disturbances $u_{2i}$ and $u_{3i}$ in both $v_{1i}$ and $v_{2i}$. Thus we have a non-linear-in-parameters generalised least squares problem, which can be solved by an appropriate numerical algorithm.

Attfield's estimates of $k_1$ and $k_2$ are 0.94 and 0.12 (standard errors 0.035 and 0.044) respectively, and the estimate of $\alpha$ is not significantly different from 1, confirming the identification of the windfall gains variable with transitory income. The estimate of $k_1$ is greater than the estimated m.p.c. out of measured income, which is 0.76, in accordance with the arguments given above. The main interest lies in the estimate of $k_2$, which is significantly different from zero and so suggests that these data do not support the hypothesis of a zero m.p.c. out of transitory income, casting doubt on one element of the permanent income hypothesis.

## RECENT EXPERIENCE

A recent stimulus to further developments in modelling the aggregate consumption-income relation has been the change in the average propensity to consume since the early 1970's. Figure 3, reproduced from Townend's (1976) paper in the *Bank of England Quarterly Bulletin*, shows consumers' expenditure on non-durables and saving, each expressed as a percentage of personal disposable income (all seasonally adjusted) over the period 1960-1975. During the 1960's the a.p.c. shows a slight secular decrease and the savings ratio a slight increase, but when trend lines fitted to the period 1960-1971 (solid lines) are projected, an inadequate explanation of the changes experienced in the period 1972-1975 is obtained. The rate of personal saving in this period is unusually high and consumers' expenditure correspondingly low.

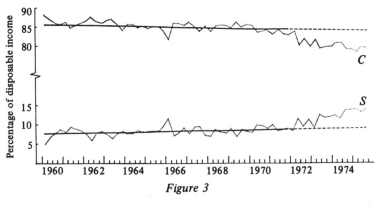

*Figure 3*

These changes were not predicted by the aggregate consumption function estimates available at the time. Townend reports that typical dynamic consumption-income relations fitted to data up to the end of 1973 exhibit substantial, persistently negative forecast errors when used to predict through 1974 and 1975: consumers' expenditure is regularly over-predicted by such equations. Likewise the consumption function of Davidson *et al.* (1978) discussed above (p.12), which was fitted to data up to the end of 1970, fails to capture subsequent behaviour, as indicated in Figure 4. The solid line in the chart shows the sample-period residuals (1959II-1970IV) and the forecast errors (1971I-1975IV). Recalling that the dependent variable is $\Delta_4 \log C_t$, which can be written as $\log(1 + (C_t - C_{t-4})/C_{t-4})$, and again using the approximation $\log(1+x) = x$ for small values of $x$, we see that the vertical scale is measured in proportional annual growth rates. Thus a forecast error of $-0.02$ implies that the fitted equation is overestimating the annual growth rate of consumption by two percentage points, and this is typically the case in 1974 and 1975.

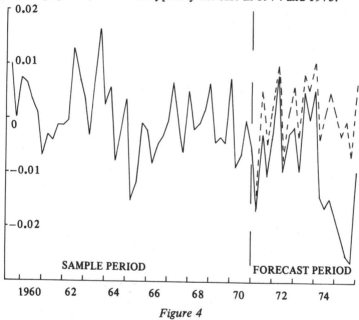

*Figure 4*

In the face of this apparent discontinuity one might simply assume that the consumption-income relationship takes a different form from 1973 onwards and, once sufficient data become available, attempt to establish the "new" form. However a sequence of different models, each valid for only a short period of time, represents an unsatisfactory state of affairs for economic analysis and policy, and it is more constructive to use the new experience to seek an improved model that provides a better explanation of consumer behaviour throughout the whole period.

## LIQUID ASSETS AND WEALTH

Allowance for the roles of wealth and liquid assets in the consumption function is not novel, but in the present context Townend (1976) finds that whereas the wealth data then available offer no improvement on the simpler consumption functions, the inclusion of a liquid assets variable ameliorates the poor forecasting performance described above.

Wealth has a direct role in the life-cycle hypothesis of Modigliani according to which all resources of the consumer are relevant to consumption decisions, wealth serving to balance income variations over time. In this model the consumer allocates income so as to maximise utility over his lifetime, and the "purpose of saving is to enable the household to redistribute the resources it gets (and expects to get) over its life cycle in order to secure the most desirable pattern of consumption over life" (Modigliani and Ando, 1957, p.105). In Friedman's theoretical model permanent income is given by wealth times the rate of return at which wealth is discounted, although as we have seen permanent income is subsequently estimated from current and past observed income. Thus in either model one might wish to consider the influence of actual wealth on consumption decisions, by introducing wealth as an explanatory variable in the consumption function. However if wealth data are not available, or are available relatively infrequently, liquid assets might be used as a proxy variable. Moreover liquid assets may be the element of wealth most relevant to consumption plans. An alternative view suggests that holdings of liquid assets are an important determinant of consumer behaviour through a portfolio balance effect: if liquid asset holdings are at their desired level, then consumption plans will be carried out, but if they are insufficient with respect to this position having in mind both precautionary and transactions motives, then expenditure will be reduced.

Townend enters the real stock of net liquid assets held by the personal sector as an explanatory variable in the non-durables consumption function, and finds that the new variable is statistically significant. Moreover, when the new equation estimated up to the end of 1973 is used to predict through 1975 there is considerable improvement, and in particular the forecast errors are no longer consistently negative. Townend gives a careful treatment of income from current grants from public authorities (national insurance benefits, family allowances, assistance grants, and so forth) since such income might be expected to be consumed more rapidly than other income, but otherwise the fitted equations are the lagged dependent variable forms discussed above (p.22), with $X$ representing the liquid assets variable, and there is an attempt to distinguish between partial adjustment and adaptive expectations/permanent income formulations. This is carried out in the context of estimation subject to an autoregressive error term, although as noted previously a moving average error specification is more appropriate for the permanent income model: nevertheless his significant *negative* autocorrelation does offer some evidence in support of the permanent income framework. Our own estimates[1] from Townend's data, subject to a moving average error and the restrictions implied by the use of the Koyck transformation, are

$$C_t = 0.640 \, C_{t-1} + 0.165 \, Y_t + 0.045 \, X_t$$
$$(.042) \qquad (.021) \qquad (.007)$$

$$- \, 0.640 \times 0.045 \, X_{t-1} + \epsilon_t - 0.640 \, \epsilon_{t-1}.$$

(The equation also contains a constant term, quarterly dummy variables, and dummy variables to represent the switch in expenditure in early 1968, as in Davidson *et al.*, and a similar switch in early 1973 before the introduction of value-added tax: for simplicity these coefficients are not reported.) Coefficients for which no standard error is given are constrained in estimation, and a likelihood ratio test indicates that the null hypothesis that these constraints are true is not rejected by these data. Thus the data offer support for a permanent income view of the consumption function. As far as the liquid assets effect is concerned Townend's conclusion, based on tests for a structural break, is that its significance applies "not merely to the latest observations but also from the beginning of the estimation period in the mid-1960's".

[1] Using a program written by Dr D. R. Osborn.

## INFLATION EFFECTS

Since the rate of inflation in the early 1970's was considerably greater than that experienced previously, explanations of the breakdown of previous models have also been based on their omission of the effects of inflation. Keynes postulates that "the consumption of the wealth-owning class may be extremely susceptible to unforeseen changes in the money-value of its wealth", and Tyrni (1964) presents a model in which, in the face of a fall in the real value of bonds caused by a rise in prices, consumers try to compensate for the loss by saving more. Since Townend enters the *real* stock of liquid assets into his consumption function his results can also be interpreted in this light, however Tyrni reports a *direct* positive effect of the inflation rate on changes in the savings ratio over the period 1949-1960.

Deaton (1977) presents a model in which changes in the savings ratio are related directly to unanticipated inflation. Because consumer goods are bought sequentially, the consumer does not have accurate up-to-date information on the prices of all goods, but merely on the prices of those goods actually purchased. Thus the consumer cannot distinguish relative price changes from absolute price changes, at least in the short run. If prices are expected to have risen by say one per cent over a given period but have actually risen by two per cent then the consumer may conclude, erroneously, that those commodities he intends to buy are relatively expensive and so he actually buys less of them than initially intended. This mistake is only discovered after the full range of prices has been observed. "A similar situation faces other consumers so that, at any given moment of time, different individuals are engaged in the purchase of different commodities, and each finds that the price of that commodity is higher than expected, while none at that instant has enough information to calculate the absolute price level. Consequently, there is a mass illusion that all goods are relatively more expensive so that, as each consumer attempts to adjust his purchases, real consumption falls, and if real income is maintained, the saving ratio rises. Certainly, as mistakes are discovered, attempts will be made to rectify them, but if inflation continues to accelerate and if expectations lag behind reality, the saving ratio will remain abnormally high." (Deaton, 1977, p.899).

Such effects are formalised in Deaton's theoretical model, which results in the relation

$$\frac{S}{Y} = \frac{S^*}{Y^*} + \left\{ \log\left(\frac{Y}{P}\right) - \log\left(\frac{Y^*}{P^*}\right) \right\} - \phi\left\{ \log P - \log P^* \right\},$$

where $Y$ and $S$ are money income and saving, respectively, $P$ is the aggregate price level, and asterisks denote anticipated or planned values. This is a *disequilibrium* model, consistent with any equilibrium consumption or savings function, which is represented by the first term on the right-hand side of the equation. The second term states that all unanticipated real income is saved, which is inevitable in this model given the consumer's sequential planning procedure. The third term describes the inflation effect on saving. The theoretical derivation implies that the coefficient $\phi$ is negative, thus if real income is correctly anticipated, possibly as a result of either wage inflation or indexation, unanticipated inflation causes the saving ratio to rise. Notice that this is the reverse of the traditional money illusion effect, according to which consumers are more sensitive to changes in nominal income than prices, so that identical increases in income and prices lead to increased consumption and lower saving.

Deaton bases a regression equation on the above relation, and estimates it from British and American data over a twenty-year span from the mid-1950s to the mid-1970s. A significant inflation effect, with the hypothesised sign, is found in both countries. When the sample period is split into two halves the inflation variable retains its sign and significance in both halves, thus the estimated inflation effect is not merely an artefact of the recent experience, yet its magnitude is such as to provide a good explanation of that experience. The effect is of similar magnitude in both countries, and implies that when the quarterly rate of inflation is running at 2% above the anticipated rate, slightly more than 1% of disposable income is involuntarily saved.

Unanticipated inflation, the difference between actual and expected inflation, is the key variable in this model, thus inflation expectations play a crucial role, despite their unobservable nature. The lack of data on expectations is typically overcome by assumptions about the mechanism by which expectations are formed or about the outcome of such a mechanism, and Deaton's basic results are obtained under the assumption that anticipated inflation is constant throughout the sample period. Although unrealistic this may only be unreasonable for the most recent observations, and Deaton's attempts to generalise this simple assumption met with little success. Nevertheless the effect of the assumption is that *actual* inflation becomes the key variable, and expected inflation is subsumed in the constant term of the regression equation.

Given this evidence other investigators have included inflation effects in their models, and in particular Davidson *et al.* (1978) obtain the following results when the model presented above (p.12) is modified in this way:

$$\Delta_4 \log C_t = 0.47 \, \Delta_4 \log Y_t - 0.21 \, \Delta_1\Delta_4 \log Y_t - 0.10 \log (C/Y)_{t-4}$$
$$\quad (0.04) \qquad\qquad (0.05) \qquad\qquad\quad (0.02)$$

$$- 0.13 \, \Delta_4 \log P_t - 0.28 \, \Delta_1\Delta_4 \log P_t + 0.01 \, \Delta_4 \log D_t.$$
$$\quad (0.07) \qquad\qquad (0.15) \qquad\qquad (0.003)$$

The inflation terms are jointly significant, confirming Deaton's result that inflation was significantly reducing consumers' expenditure prior to 1971. They also lead to a striking improvement in forecast performance, as indicated by the dotted line in Figure 4, which gives the forecast errors of the new equation. We see that the persistent overestimation of consumption in 1974 and 1975 is no longer a feature. (To avoid confusing the picture the sample-period residuals of the new equation are not plotted in the figure, as they are rather close to the sample-period residuals already plotted.) Again calculating the implied consumption-income relation on a steady-state growth path with annual real growth rate $g$ and inflation rate $\pi$ (that is, $\Delta_4 \log P_t = \pi$), we obtain

$$\log C^e - \log Y^e = (-0.53g - 0.13\pi)/0.10,$$

or $C^e = kY^e$ where $k = \exp(-5.3g - 1.3\pi)$. With $g = 0.02$ and $\pi = 0.05$, as was approximately true during the sample period, the a.p.c. is given by $k = 0.84$, exactly the same value as in the previous model. When $\pi$ increases to 0.15, the consumption-income ratio falls to 0.74, both values characterising the early 1970's.

By virtue of its increased explanatory power during the sample period, its acceptable forecasting performance after the "break", and long-run properties consonant with established theory, this dynamic model is an improvement on its forerunners. At first sight the experience of the early 1970's seems to have had an impact similar to that of the immediate post-war period discussed previously (pp.4-7): the behaviour of key variables changed substantially, existing models broke down, theoretical and empirical improvements were made, and new models resulted that provide a better explanation of consumer behaviour throughout the whole period. However the impact of inflation on household behaviour, and indeed on national income statistical practice, is by no means a closed subject, and in applied econometrics there is no such thing as the last word.

# II

# THE PRODUCTION FUNCTION

### INTRODUCTION

We begin our study of the production function with a brief review of the relevant economic theory. The traditional theory begins with two inputs, capital and labour, denoted $K$ and $L$, which are continuously variable and continuously substitutable in production at all times; this takes us away from the realm of linear production models with fixed coefficients. To each combination of capital and labour there corresponds a unique maximum quantity of output, $Q$:

$$Q = F(K,L).$$

In effect the production function is a technical relation in flow terms, flows of services from stocks of labour and capital combining to produce a flow of output. The function summarises the efficient production possibilities open to a firm, a technical maximisation problem having been solved.

It is conventional to distinguish between capital and labour inputs, but the above representation in terms of only two inputs is a gross over-simplification, for there are of course many varieties of capital and labour inputs. These can be combined into single aggregate variables provided that the marginal rate of substitution between any two kinds of one factor is independent of any variety of the other factor, and these aggregate variables can be treated as if they were actual individual inputs provided that they are linear homogeneous functions of the different varieties. (We shall remind ourselves of these technical terms in a moment.) Thus an aggregation problem arises even at the level of an individual firm, long before the question of the aggregation of equations in industry studies arises — it is only avoided at the extreme micro level of one man with one machine. In practice we tend to make the heroic assumption that the above necessary conditions are satisfied more often than we acknowledge heterogeneity by introducing sub-categories of $K$ and $L$ as subsidiary arguments in the production function.

At first we shall assume the function to be fixed although in due course we shall allow it to shift in some way, for example, due to (disembodied) technical change, which poses the problem of distinguishing movements along a given production function from shifts of the function, the basic problem in estimating technical progress. Since the production function is a mere summary of technical constraints, by itself it allows for no testing of economic hypotheses. Actual observed data are the results of economic decisions in which the production function is but one constraint. Thus production functions are used in conjunction with marginal productivity theory to provide explanations of factor prices and the levels of factor utilisation, and so at a theoretical level play a central role in the analysis of growth and distribution. This analysis is discussed at the macro level, while at the micro level questions of substitution possibilities and economies of scale arise. The available data correspond to reduced form observations and raise familiar identification problems, for the production function is embedded in a simultaneous equations model and cannot be identified if, for example, the marginal productivity conditions are not distinguishable from it. We shall be treating situations in which economic agents are assumed to have solved their technical problems, and examine inputs, outputs, prices and so on making various assumptions about the nature of the economic system in which the firm or entrepreneur operates. The questions that have been most frequently addressed to the data that result from this process concern the extent of economies of scale, substitutability of factors, and technical progress.

## PROPERTIES OF THE NEOCLASSICAL PRODUCTION FUNCTION

The production function $Q = F(K,L)$, defined on $K \geq 0$, $L \geq 0$, is single-valued, continuous, and (at least) twice differentiable. Denoting partial derivatives by

$$\frac{\partial Q}{\partial K} = F_K, \frac{\partial^2 Q}{\partial K^2} = F_{KK},$$

and so forth, we assume

$$F_K > 0, F_L > 0, F_{KK} < 0, F_{LL} < 0$$

ensuring marginal products which are positive and decreasing.

An *isoquant* diagram shows the function $Q = F(K,L)$ for a given output level, and thus shows the different input combinations giving

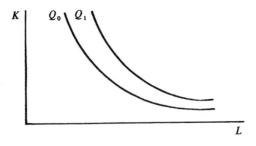

*Figure 5*

rise to the same output (Figure 5). Taking the total differential of $Q = F(K,L)$ along an isoquant ($Q$ constant) gives

$$dQ = F_K dK + F_L dL = 0.$$

Output does not change as we move along an isoquant, hence the absolute value of the slope of the isoquant, the *marginal rate of substitution R*, is given by

$$R = -\frac{dK}{dL} = \frac{F_L}{F_K}.$$

This is assumed to decrease as substitution proceeds, giving an isoquant convex to the origin. The *elasticity of substitution*, σ, is a further parameter of interest. It is defined as the proportionate change in the factor input ratio as a result of a proportionate change in the marginal rate of substitution, and measures the ease of substitution between factors.

$$\sigma = \frac{d \log (K/L)}{d \log R} > 0.$$

A value of zero indicates that no substitution is possible — factors are combined in a fixed proportion.

The production function is commonly assumed to be *homogeneous*, in which case we can write

$$F(hK,hL) = h^\nu F(K,L) = h^\nu Q \,,$$

and the degree of homogeneity, $\nu$, is a parameter of considerable interest. On increasing capital and labour inputs by the factor $h$, output increases by the factor $h^\nu$: a value of $\nu = 1$ indicates constant returns to scale, and increasing or decreasing returns are indicated by values greater than or less than unity. An important property of homogeneous functions is given by Euler's theorem, obtained by differentiating the above relation with respect to $h$ and then setting $h$ equal to unity. The theorem states that the sum of the first partial derivates weighted by the factor quantities is equal to output times the degree of homogeneity:

$$F_K K + F_L L = \nu Q \,.$$

As an illustration take the case of $\nu = 1$, namely a *linear* homogeneous production function, exhibiting constant returns to scale. Then

$$F_K K + F_L L = Q$$

so that if factors are paid their marginal products then the product is exhausted: there are no pure losses or profits. The linear homogeneous function is equivalent to a function of one variable in *per capita* terms. Setting $h = 1/L$, we have

$$Q/L = F(K/L, L/L).$$

Denoting output *per capita* $Q/L$ by $q$, the capital-labour ratio $K/L$ by $k$, and the function $F(k, 1)$ by $f(k)$, we can write

$$q = f(k).$$

The marginal product conditions become $dq/dk > 0$, $d^2 q/dk^2 < 0$, and if these are satisfied the *per capita* production function can be represented as in Figure 6.

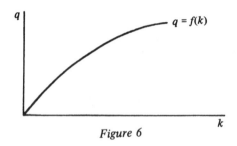

*Figure 6*

## THE COBB-DOUGLAS PRODUCTION FUNCTION

A convenient and widely-used illustration is provided by the Cobb-Douglas production function, namely

$$Q = AK^{\alpha}L^{\beta}.$$

The degree of homogeneity is $\alpha + \beta$ since

$$F(hK,hL) = A(hK)^{\alpha}(hL)^{\beta} = h^{\alpha+\beta} AK^{\alpha}L^{\beta} = h^{\alpha+\beta}Q.$$

Hence the Cobb-Douglas production function exhibits constant returns to scale when $\alpha + \beta = 1$, in which case it can be written in *per capita* terms as $q = Ak^\alpha$. The marginal products are obtained by differentiation:

$$\frac{\partial Q}{\partial K} = \alpha AK^{\alpha-1}L^\beta = \alpha \frac{Q}{K}, \frac{\partial Q}{\partial L} = \beta AK^\alpha L^{\beta-1} = \beta \frac{Q}{L},$$

thus the parameters $\alpha$ and $\beta$ give the elasticities of output with respect to capital and labour, respectively. The second partial derivatives are

$$\frac{\partial^2 Q}{\partial K^2} = \alpha(\alpha-1)AK^{\alpha-2}L^\beta = \alpha(\alpha-1)\frac{Q}{K^2},$$

$$\frac{\partial^2 Q}{\partial L^2} = \beta(\beta-1)AK^\alpha L^{\beta-2} = \beta(\beta-1)\frac{Q}{L^2},$$

thus marginal products are positive and decreasing if $0 < \alpha < 1$, $0 < \beta < 1$.

The marginal rate of substitution of capital for labour is

$$R = \frac{\partial Q}{\partial L} / \frac{\partial Q}{\partial K} = \beta \frac{Q}{L} / \alpha \frac{Q}{K} = \frac{\beta}{\alpha} \frac{K}{L}.$$

To derive the elasticity of substitution we write this equation as

$$\log R = \log \frac{\beta}{\alpha} + \log \frac{K}{L},$$

hence

$$\sigma = \frac{d \log (K/L)}{d \log R} = 1.$$

Thus for the Cobb-Douglas production function the elasticity of substitution does not vary with the combination of factors used, and is equal to unity everywhere.

## THE ECONOMIC MODEL

We now examine a simple economic model of the behaviour of the firm. The production function is a *technical* relation between output and inputs, acting as a constraint on the firm's choice of output and input levels, which otherwise result from *economic* decisions. Thus in general the observed values of prices, output and inputs are generated by a set of simultaneous relationships, and so it is inappropriate to estimate the production function as a single regression equation treating capital and labour as exogenous variables. The simplest case is given by assuming perfect competition in product and factor markets, which means that the prices of output ($p$), capital ($r$) and labour ($w$) are predetermined: the firm is a price-taker.

We first consider the cost-minimisation problem, and shall shortly examine a cost function study. For a given level of output $Q$, determined exogenously by demand conditions, say, the firm is assumed to choose its input levels $K$ and $L$ so as to minimise total costs

$$TC = rK + wL$$

subject to $Q = F(K,L)$. The Lagrangean function is

$$\mathcal{L} = rK + wL - \lambda\big\{Q - F(K,L)\big\}.$$

The first order conditions are

$$\frac{\partial \mathcal{L}}{\partial K} = r + \lambda F_K = 0$$

$$\frac{\partial \mathcal{L}}{\partial L} = w + \lambda F_L = 0$$

so that

$$\frac{F_L}{F_K} = \frac{w}{r},$$

and

$$\frac{\partial \mathcal{L}}{\partial \lambda} = -Q + F(K,L) = 0,$$

ensuring that the firm remains on its production function. Thus the optimal solution occurs when the marginal rate of substitution is equal to the factor price ratio, and in this context (cost-minimising price-takers) the elasticity of substitution is given as

$$\sigma = \frac{d \log(K/L)}{d \log(w/r)},$$

the percentage change in the capital-labour ratio in response to a one percent change in the factor price ratio. Solving the above two conditions gives the cost-minimising input levels in terms of their prices and the given output level. Substituting these into the expression for *TC* gives the minimum total cost as a function of $r$, $w$ and $Q$. This function is simply termed the cost function; it is the dual of the production function.

*Example*

For the Cobb-Douglas production function

$$Q = AK^{\alpha}L^{\beta}$$

we have

$$\frac{F_L}{F_K} = \frac{\beta}{\alpha}\frac{K}{L} = \frac{w}{r}.$$

From this we obtain the relation

$$L = \frac{\beta}{\alpha}\frac{r}{w}K$$

which can be substituted into the production function to give

$$Q = A K^{\alpha+\beta} \left[\frac{\beta}{\alpha}\frac{r}{w}\right]^{\beta}$$

so that on rearranging the cost-minimising level of capital input is given by

$$K = \left[\frac{Q}{A}\right]^{1/\nu} \left[\frac{\beta}{\alpha}\frac{r}{w}\right]^{-\beta/\nu}$$

where $\nu = \alpha+\beta$ is the degree of returns to scale. Similarly, for labour input:

$$L = \left[\frac{Q}{A}\right]^{1/\nu} \left[\frac{\alpha}{\beta}\frac{w}{r}\right]^{-\alpha/\nu}.$$

The cost function is then obtained as

$$TC = rK + wL$$

$$= \left[\frac{Q}{A}\right]^{1/\nu} \left\{ r\left[\frac{\beta}{\alpha}\frac{r}{w}\right]^{-\beta/\nu} + w\left[\frac{\alpha}{\beta}\frac{w}{r}\right]^{-\alpha/\nu} \right\}$$

$$= k\, Q^{1/\nu}\, r^{\alpha/\nu}\, w^{\beta/\nu},$$

where the constant $k$ is given by

$$k = A^{-1/\nu}\, (\alpha^{\beta/\nu}\, \beta^{-\beta/\nu} + \alpha^{-\alpha/\nu}\, \beta^{\alpha/\nu})$$

$$= A^{-1/\nu}\, (\alpha+\beta)(\alpha^\alpha\beta^\beta)^{-1/\nu}$$

$$= \nu(A\alpha^\alpha\beta^\beta)^{-1/\nu}.$$

Thus the cost function is log-linear in output and factor prices:

$$\log TC = \log k + \frac{1}{\nu}\log Q + \frac{\alpha}{\nu}\log r + \frac{\beta}{\nu}\log w.$$

In the *profit maximisation* problem the quantity of output to be produced is also a decision variable, and the problem is to choose the levels of output and inputs which maximise profits. Since costs must be minimised if profits are to be maximised, the problem is simply to maximise

$$\Pi = pQ - TC(Q,r,w)$$

with respect to $Q$ — there is no constraint as the production function is incorporated in the derivation of $TC$. The first order condition $\partial\Pi/\partial Q = 0$ yields the familiar requirement that price equals marginal cost and the second order condition for a maximum is $\partial^2\Pi/\partial Q^2 < 0$, that is $\partial^2 TC/\partial Q^2 > 0$, or marginal cost should be increasing. Having obtained the profit-maximising level of $Q$ from the first-order condition, the input levels then follow from the preceding cost-minimising input functions; substituting the optimal value of $Q$ in terms of $p$, $r$, and $w$ into these functions gives the derived demand functions for $K$ and $L$, which are functions only of prices.

Alternatively, the profit-maximising values of $Q$, $K$, and $L$ can be obtained in a single calculation by maximising

$$\Pi = pQ - rK - wL$$

subject to $Q = F(K,L)$. The Lagrangean function is

$$\mathcal{L} = pQ - rK - wL - \lambda\{Q - F(K,L)\}$$

and the first-order conditions are

$$\frac{\partial\mathcal{L}}{\partial Q} = p - \lambda = 0$$

$$\frac{\partial\mathcal{L}}{\partial K} = -r + \lambda F_K = 0 \quad \text{hence } r = pF_K,$$

$$\frac{\partial\mathcal{L}}{\partial L} = -w + \lambda F_L = 0 \quad \text{hence } w = pF_L.$$

The two equations on the right are the *marginal productivity conditions*: for each input the value of its marginal product must equal its price, and solving these together with $Q = F(K,L)$ yields the profit-maximising levels of $Q$, $K$, and $L$.

*Example*

In the Cobb-Douglas case the marginal productivity conditions are

$$r = p\frac{\alpha Q}{K} \quad \text{and} \quad w = p\frac{\beta Q}{L},$$

thus $\alpha = rK/pQ$ and $\beta = wL/pQ$ can be interpreted as the respective shares of capital and labour in total output. The firm's optimal output and input levels result from solving these two equations together with $Q = AK^\alpha L^\beta$. Writing in logarithmic form, the equations are

$$\log Q = \log A + \alpha \log K + \beta \log L$$

$$\log Q + \log \alpha = \log K + \log \frac{r}{p}$$

$$\log Q + \log \beta = \log L + \log \frac{w}{p}$$

or, rearranging,

$$
\begin{bmatrix}
1 & -\alpha & -\beta \\
1 & -1 & 0 \\
1 & 0 & -1
\end{bmatrix}
\begin{bmatrix}
\log Q \\
\log K \\
\log L
\end{bmatrix}
=
\begin{bmatrix}
\log A \\
\log \dfrac{r}{p} - \log \alpha \\
\log \dfrac{w}{p} - \log \beta
\end{bmatrix}.
$$

A solution for (the logarithms of) $Q$, $K$ and $L$, giving the reduced form of the system, can be obtained provided that the determinant of the coefficient matrix is not zero. This determinant is equal to $1 - \alpha - \beta$, and three cases arise according to whether this is positive, zero, or negative, that is whether there are decreasing, constant, or increasing returns to scale.

First, in the case of constant returns to scale the coefficient matrix is singular and there is no unique solution. Either the first-order conditions are incompatible, that is the system of equations is inconsistent and there is *no* solution, or if the exogenous variables $p$, $r$ and $w$ happen to have suitable values, there is an infinite number of solutions. Equally we may consider the problem posed initially of maximising $\Pi = pQ - TC(Q,r,w)$ with respect to $Q$, and obtain the first-order condition when $v=1$ as

$$p - kr^\alpha w^{1-\alpha} = 0.$$

In general the exogenous price variables cannot be expected to satisfy this relation, and so there is no solution. Marginal cost does not depend on the level of output, and if it happens by chance that the price of output and marginal cost are equal, then the first-order condition is satisfied at any level of output and there are infinitely many solutions.

Secondly, if there are non-constant returns to scale, $\alpha+\beta\neq1$, a unique solution to the necessary first-order conditions exists, and we must now check the second-order conditions for maximum profit. These are obtained most easily by considering the problem of maximising $\Pi = pF(K,L) - rK - wL$ with respect to $K$ and $L$, having eliminated the constraint by substitution. Since the second and third terms in this expression are linear in $K$ and $L$, the second-order conditions concern only the first term. The requirement for a maximum is that the (Hessian) matrix of second partial derivatives is negative semidefinite, and this gives the conditions

$$F_{KK} < 0, F_{LL} < 0, F_{KK}F_{LL} - (F_{KL})^2 > 0.$$

The first two conditions are satisfied if $0 < \alpha < 1$ and $0 < \beta < 1$, as we have seen, and the third implies

$$\alpha\beta(\alpha-1)(\beta-1)\frac{Q^2}{K^2L^2} - \left(\alpha\beta\frac{Q}{KL}\right)^2 > 0,$$

or $\alpha + \beta < 1$. Thus in order for the marginal productivity conditions to have a determinate solution corresponding to maximum profit, there must be *decreasing* returns to scale. Constant or increasing returns to scale are incompatible with the assumption of both perfect competition and profit maximisation.

Two observations can be made about this conclusion. First, it seems unreasonable to rule out constant or increasing returns as a technical characteristic of the production function, certainly in advance of any empirical work. Secondly, indeterminacy of $Q$, $K$, and $L$ is unrealistic: in practice these variables do take definite values. So it becomes necessary to consider models other than that of a profit maximiser choosing output and input levels with prices given. For example, and looking ahead a little, increasing returns are compatible with cost minimisation in a regulated industry. Or the assumption of perfectly elastic input supply and output demand might be relaxed by adding factor supply or product demand functions. In this case one or more prices become endogenous variables, leading to a more extensive system, but in such a system increasing returns may not be incompatible with profit maximisation. Thus it is necessary to consider carefully the institutional arrangements, behavioural hypotheses, and so forth that are represented in a model, lest an injudicious choice of model automatically precludes or is inconsistent with certain observable economic phenomena.

## THE STATISTICAL MODEL

Further problems arise when we seek to formulate an appropriate statistical model for estimation and testing. We first consider the random disturbance terms incorporated in the model to account for variations in the data. Assume that we have data on a cross-section of firms, that the coefficients $\alpha$ and $\beta$ do not differ from firm to firm, but the efficiency with which a given input combination is utilised is subject to random variation. Then for the $i$th firm we can write

$$Q_i = A \, K_i^{\alpha} L_i^{\beta} \, e^{u_{1i}}.$$

The disturbance is written in this exponential form so that the symbol $u$ retains its previous interpretation as a zero-mean random variable, taking positive and negative values. The random variable $\exp(u)$ is always positive, taking values above and below one, and if $u$ is normally distributed $\exp(u)$ is said to be log-normally distributed. The disturbance term represents the *technical* or *productive efficiency* of the firm — its knowledge, skill, locational advantages, luck, effort, and so forth. In effect the multiplicative factor in the production function has become $A \exp(u_{1i})$, and the position (but not the shape) of a particular isoquant is subject to random variation. Error terms are also introduced into the marginal productivity conditions:

$$\alpha \frac{Q_i}{K_i} = \frac{r}{p} e^{u_{2i}} \,,\, \beta \frac{Q_i}{L_i} = \frac{w}{p} e^{u_{3i}}.$$

These factors reflect the firm's *economic* or *commercial efficiency*, that is its ability to achieve the profit-maximising position, and any departure from $u_{2i} = u_{3i} = 0$ implies less-than-maximum profits.

Let us now consider the complete stochastic model relevant to the situation implicit in the above marginal productivity conditions, namely that of profit maximisation with given prices. Assume that there are *decreasing* returns to scale, to avoid the problems of the previous section. Writing the (logarithms of) endogenous variables on the left-hand side, we have

$$\log Q_i - \alpha \log K_i - \beta \log L_i = \log A \qquad\qquad + u_{1i}$$
$$\log Q_i - \phantom{\alpha} \log K_i \qquad\qquad = \log (r/p) - \log \alpha + u_{2i}$$
$$\log Q_i \qquad\qquad - \phantom{\beta} \log L_i = \log (w/p) - \log \beta + u_{3i}$$

In accordance with the assumption of perfect competition, all firms in the cross-section are assumed to face the same prices, hence these are written without subscripts: the prices are constants, not variables. This immediately implies that the production function is not identified when it is estimated as a single equation. Since the right-hand sides of the three equations contain only constants and random disturbances, the first equation is indistinguishable from an arbitrary linear combination of the three equations. In effect one would be attempting to estimate the shape of an isoquant, but identical firms facing the same prices will choose inputs in the same ratio, except for purely random variation, and hence be randomly distributed around the same point on the isoquant: such observations are not informative about the shape of the isoquant.

A number of possible ways of overcoming this difficulty have been proposed. First, there may be cases in which prices do vary across the sample, possibly as a result of regional differences or factor immobility. (Such variation is present in the data used in Nerlove's study discussed below.) Of course time series data will generally exhibit price variation, but the static nature of the present formulation is then likely to become an additional shortcoming, requiring consideration of optimisation over time, for example, and of the fact that investment does not occur instantaneously, as discussed in the next chapter. Also, as noted in the preceding section, price variation might result from non-competitive conditions, but this requires the specification of demand or supply functions, one or more prices becoming endogenous variables in a larger system of equations.

Secondly, in the constant-price context, estimation might be based on the second and third equations of the system. Notice that if $(r/p)$ and $(w/p)$ are observed so that the first term on the right-hand side is kept separate from the "intercept" term $\log \alpha$ or $\log \beta$, then there are non-linear restrictions on the parameters of the system, namely that these intercept terms are the logarithms of the coefficients in the first equation. Such non-linear restrictions across equations preclude the application of the standard rank and order conditions for identifiability, nevertheless $\alpha$ and $\beta$ are identified in the last two equations, and this is the basis of Klein's estimation from factor shares, discussed below.

Finally, if price information is not available or is ignored, so that the non-linear restriction on the intercept terms does not hold, identification might be achieved by restrictions on error covariances. For example, technical efficiency and economic efficiency might be assumed to be uncorrelated, that is, $E(u_{1i} u_{2i}) = E(u_{1i} u_{3i}) = 0$. This might be relevant in agriculture, where input decisions and output realisations are separated by the passage of time, and where the disturbance terms capture the effect of distinct influences, for example, climatic influences in the case of the output disturbance. Then a linear combination including the last two equations could be distinguished from the production function, for it would have an error term containing and hence correlated with $u_2$ and/or $u_3$, unlike the production function itself. In effect, data on $\log Q_i$, $\log K_i$ and $\log L_i$ in mean deviation form permit estimation of the variances and covariances of these variables, and these six quantities are given by the model as functions of $\alpha$, $\beta$, the three error variances, and $E(u_{2i} u_{3i})$, which are thus estimable: the restriction $E(u_{1i} u_{2i}) = E(u_{1i} u_{3i}) = 0$ reduces the number of unknowns by two, identifying the remaining six.

## REDUCED FORM ESTIMATION: RETURNS TO SCALE IN ELECTRICITY SUPPLY

The cross-section study of public utility enterprises by Nerlove (1963) is an interesting example of the incorporation of the specific features of an industry into an empirical model. When formulated to accommodate the available data, this yields an answer to the question of the extent of increasing returns to scale in the generation of electric power in the United States. The identification problems discussed above are avoided by working with a reduced form equation: the cost function derived previously (p.46) is not only a reduced form equation of the relevant model, but also a convenient form for empirical implementation, given what variables can and cannot be observed.

The particular features of the electricity supply industry that are relevant are as follows.

1. Power is supplied on demand and cannot be stored. Hence output ($Q$) is beyond the firm's control, and can be treated as an exogenous variable.
2. Rates (prices) are set by the utility commission so that $p$ is predetermined: 1 and 2 together imply that total revenue is predetermined.
3. Labour is unionised with wage rates set by long-term contracts so that the individual firm is a price-taker in the short-run labour market. (In the long run it might be assumed that the contracts are in fact competitive, but this assumption is not required.)
4. Capital markets are assumed highly competitive.
5. Fuel contracts are long term and competitively priced so that the firm is again a price-taker in the short run.

Assumptions 3, 4 and 5 imply that factor prices are given to a particular firm, but they are not identical across the whole industry. Such

variation in prices permits the estimation of a cost function across
> firms. Adding assumptions 1 and 2 (*pQ* predetermined) implies that
profit-maximisation is equivalent to cost minimisation, so the analysis
of p.44 is relevant. Taking a Cobb-Douglas production function, the
> cost-minimising input functions derived on p.46 are *reduced form*
equations under these assumptions, and the cost function is simply a
linear combination of these, giving endogenous total costs in terms of
exogenous input prices and output: data are available on all of these
variables. An advantage of this approach is that data are not required on
physical inputs, which are often difficult to measure.

The Cobb-Douglas production function is slightly generalised to the
case of three inputs, as follows:

$$Q = A x_1^{\alpha_1} x_2^{\alpha_2} x_3^{\alpha_3}$$

where $x_1$ is the amount of labour input, $x_2$ the amount of capital
input, and $x_3$ the amount of fuel input ($p_i$, $i=1,2,3$ denoting their
respective prices). A derivation as on p.46 then leads to the generalised
cost function

$$\log TC = \log k + \frac{1}{\nu} \log Q + \frac{\alpha_1}{\nu} \log p_1 + \frac{\alpha_2}{\nu} \log p_2 + \frac{\alpha_3}{\nu} \log p_3$$

where

$$\nu = \alpha_1 + \alpha_2 + \alpha_3$$

and

$$k = \nu \left( A \alpha_1^{\alpha_1} \alpha_2^{\alpha_2} \alpha_3^{\alpha_3} \right)^{-1/\nu}.$$

The four variables on the right-hand side are all predetermined, and a
direct estimate of the degree of returns to scale is possible. A slight
problem is that the parameters are overidentified: the five coefficients
($k, 1/\nu, \alpha_1/\nu, \alpha_2/\nu, \alpha_3/\nu$) are functions of only four parameters ($\alpha_1, \alpha_2$,
$\alpha_3, A$). But $\alpha_1 + \alpha_2 + \alpha_3 = \nu$ and so the extra degree of freedom can be

removed by imposing this restriction on the estimates. This can be done by dividing *TC* and two prices by the remaining price, say $p_3$, that is, by subtracting $\log p_3$ from both sides. In this way Nerlove's *Model A* is derived:

$$\log TC - \log p_3 = \log k + \frac{1}{\nu} \log Q + \frac{\alpha_1}{\nu} \log p_1 + \frac{\alpha_2}{\nu} \log p_2$$

$$+ \left(\frac{\alpha_3}{\nu} - 1\right) \log p_3,$$

and as the restriction gives

$$\frac{\alpha_3}{\nu} - 1 = -\frac{\alpha_1}{\nu} - \frac{\alpha_2}{\nu}$$

we have

$$\log \frac{TC}{p_3} = \log k + \frac{1}{\nu} \log Q + \frac{\alpha_1}{\nu} \log \frac{p_1}{p_3} + \frac{\alpha_2}{\nu} \log \frac{p_2}{p_3} .$$

There are now only four coefficients, from which unique estimates of the four parameters can be derived.

This form assumes that the sample data on the prices of inputs vary across firms. Suppose the price of capital ($p_2$) does not vary. In that case $p_2$ becomes part of the constant term and the overidentification does not arise. We have *Model B*:

$$\log TC = k' + \frac{1}{\nu} \log Q + \frac{\alpha_1}{\nu} \log p_1 + \frac{\alpha_3}{\nu} \log p_3$$

where

$$k' = \log k + \frac{\alpha_2}{\nu} \log p_2 .$$

There is no need to place a restriction on this equation, since there are four coefficients giving estimates of the four parameters, an estimate of $\alpha_2$ being derived from the estimates of $\nu$, $\alpha_1$, and $\alpha_3$.

Error terms of the multiplicative type entered as above carry through to the cost function, resulting in a zero-mean additive disturbance in the log-linear regression equation. If this error term obeys the classical assumptions of independence and constant variance, then the resulting coefficient estimates are unbiased, efficient, and consistent. But the parameter estimates lose the unbiasedness property because in deriving them from the regression coefficients non-linear operations are involved. For example, to estimate $\nu$ we take the reciprocal of the coefficient of the output variable and although that coefficient provides an unbiased estimate of $1/\nu$, its reciprocal does not provide an unbiased estimate of $\nu$, for $E(1/b) \neq 1/E(b)$. So the parameter estimates only remain consistent; they are in effect indirect least squares estimates.

Nerlove had a cross-section sample of 145 firms. Previous studies had been done at the plant level, finding $\nu \geq 1$, though some reduction in returns might be expected as a number of plants are combined into a single firm. Both Models A and B found $\hat{\nu} \simeq 1.39$ and had surprisingly high $R^2$ values for cross-section studies. However this masked a number of problems, in particular $\hat{\alpha}_2$ was not significantly different from zero, which may reflect either the lack of short-run variability of capital input or other data problems with the capital price variable.

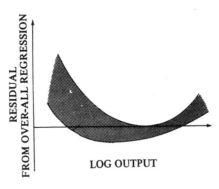

*Figure 7*

The residuals were examined to check for any systematic influence of omitted variables. Plotting them against log $Q$ showed that the residuals fell in the shaded region in Figure 7, suggesting non-constant error variance (heteroscedasticity) and a relation of residual variance to size (output of firm). This pattern is not surprising if in fact the relationship is not genuinely linear in the logarithms. As an illustration, consider the residuals obtained when a log-linear relationship is fitted to data which obey a linear relationship, as shown in Figure 8. This is drawn with arithmetic scales on both axes and assuming that the estimated log-linear equation has a coefficient less than one. As the independent variable increases, the residuals first tend to be positive, then they are all negative, and finally again all positive, instead of showing random variability throughout. Nerlove also used the

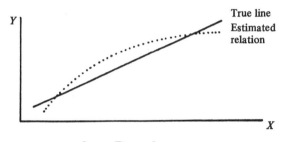

*Figure 8*

Durbin-Watson statistic. Although this is normally associated with time series data and has no obvious cross-section interpretation in general, where there does exist a meaningful ordering of the data (to correspond to the chronological ordering of time series data) it can be used as a check for mis-specification. Here the data were ordered by size of firm, as measured by output, and the Durbin-Watson statistic indicated highly significant positive serial correlation, a residual of one sign tending to be followed by another with the same sign. An economic explanation can be provided by setting up the traditional cost function, plotting $TC$ against $Q$ corresponding to a $U$-shaped long-run average cost curve. In this case $v$ is not constant and independent of $Q$ but is inversely related to it, with increasing returns at small values of $Q$ and

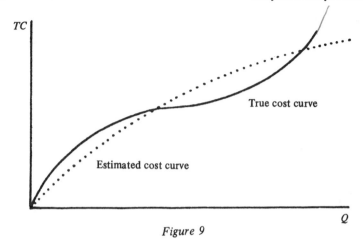

*Figure 9*

decreasing returns at large values of $Q$. If the true $TC$ function is of this type then a fitted log-linear relationship would produce the pattern of residuals found by Nerlove as it would underestimate $TC$ for small and large values of $Q$, and overestimate in the intermediate range.

Nerlove tackled this situation by splitting his sample of 145 firms into five groups of 29, ordered by output. He hoped in this way to approximate the continuous $TC$ curve by five log-linear segments. For each sub-group of firms, the total cost function was estimated, thus for each segment of the cost curve an estimate of the degree of returns to scale was obtained. Sure enough $\nu$ decreased with size of firm — smallest firms: $\hat{\nu} \simeq 2\frac{1}{2}$; medium firms: $\hat{\nu} \simeq 1\frac{1}{2}$; largest firms: $\nu$ not significantly different from 1. A test of the results is provided by comparing the residual sum of squares over the five segments with the original residual sum of squares obtained when a single relationship is assumed to hold over the whole range of output. The reduction in the residual sum of squares by stratifying the data into the five sub-groups was indeed significant. Nevertheless a problem which remained was the erratic elasticity estimates in the various segments. Nerlove's attempt to surmount this problem involved restricting the price variables in different groups to have the same coefficient and allowing only the coefficient of log $Q$ to vary. This is equivalent to imposing "neutral variations", in that marginal rates of substitution are not affected. The marginal rate of substitution of $x_i$ for $x_j$ is equal to

$$\frac{\partial Q/\partial x_j}{\partial Q/\partial x_i} = \frac{\alpha_j \, x_i}{\alpha_i \, x_j},$$

and so allowing the coefficients $\alpha_i/\nu$ to vary between groups implies that the marginal rate of substitution varies, whereas constraining the price coefficients to be the same in all groups keeps the marginal rate of substitution constant. However the data do not support this restriction, and the "neutral variation" hypothesis is rejected.

The two strong conclusions are (i) that there are variations in $\nu$ with size of firm and (ii) that there are increasing returns to scale at the firm level. In addition to illustrating the derivation and estimation of a reduced form equation under specific institutional conditions, Nerlove's study provides a good example of the value of examining residuals to test the appropriateness of a model.

## ESTIMATION FROM FACTOR SHARES

Remaining within the cross-section context we now examine an alternative to reduced form estimation introduced by Klein (1953), which is moreover applicable to situations in which there is *no* cross-sectional variation in prices, as we shall see.

In the model of p.51 comprising a Cobb-Douglas production function and two marginal productivity conditions derived from profit maximisation under perfect competition, the last two equations allow unique estimates of $\alpha$ and $\beta$ to be obtained. As an illustration we take the labour marginal productivity condition

$$\beta \frac{Q_i}{L_i} = \frac{w}{p} e^{u_{3i}},$$

which can be alternatively linearised as

$$\log \frac{wL_i}{pQ_i} = \log \beta - u_{3i}.$$

Given $n$ observations $\log \beta$ can then be estimated as the "intercept term" in this "regression equation", that is, by calculating

$$\widehat{\log} \beta = \frac{1}{n} \sum_{i=1}^{n} \log \frac{wL_i}{pQ_i} .$$

Clearly it is not necessary to have separate observations on prices and physical inputs and output, all that are required are data on factor payments and total revenue, which are often more readily available.

The properties of this estimator can be obtained as usual by substituting the right-hand side of the preceding equation into the expression for $\widehat{\log} \beta$. In particular this yields

$$E(\widehat{\log} \beta) = \log \beta - \frac{1}{n} \sum_{i=1}^{n} E(u_{3i}),$$

and so $\widehat{\log} \beta$ is an unbiased estimator of $\log \beta$ provided that the disturbance term has a zero mean. The unbiasedness property disappears when an estimate of $\beta$ itself is unscrambled by calculating $\exp(\widehat{\log} \beta)$ since this is a nonlinear operation, nevertheless the resulting estimate is consistent. The estimate is the sample *geometric* mean of labour's share in total output:

$$\hat{\beta} = \sqrt[n]{\prod_{i=1}^{n} \frac{wL_i}{pQ_i}} .$$

The assumption that marginal products are equated to factor prices is a maintained hypothesis in this calculation, and so the estimates cannot be used to test that assumption. The inferences that might be drawn from the results are further limited if a common accounting convention of assuming that all revenue is distributed to capital or labour has been followed in constructing the data. Then the data would satisfy $pQ_i = rK_i + wL_i$, and estimates of $\alpha$ and $\beta$ based on *arithmetic* mean factor shares would sum exactly to one, irrespective of the degree of returns to scale in production. The use of geometric means as above will cause the two estimates $\hat{\alpha}$ and $\hat{\beta}$ to have a sum slightly less than one in this case, but again this sum sheds no light on the question of returns to scale. In effect a fresh identification problem is posed by the use of such an accounting identity, for example to calculate the share of capital as value-added less the wage bill. Much was made of the correspondence between the least squares regression coefficients and estimated factor shares in some of the early time series studies to which we now turn, but perhaps a similar problem was present.

## TIME SERIES STUDIES

How did the early time series studies apparently turn out so well, given all the above difficulties of specifying a suitable model to enable a Cobb-Douglas production function to be identified and estimated? The results from a later study by Douglas (1948) are used by Cramer (1969, pp.234-237) to illustrate the earlier Cobb-Douglas (1928) approach. Given aggregate time series data on the three volume variables ($Q_t$, $L_t$, $K_t$), least squares estimates are calculated for the equation

$$\log Q_t = \log A + \alpha \log K_t + \beta \log L_t + u_t.$$

Typically $\hat{\alpha} + \hat{\beta} \simeq 1$, for example with U.S. data for all manufacturing industry, 1899-1922, $\hat{\alpha} = 0.25$ (s.e. 0.05) and $\hat{\beta} = 0.73$ (0.12). So constant returns to scale are imposed and the equation

$$\log \frac{Q_t}{K_t} = \log A + \beta \log \frac{L_t}{K_t} + u_t$$

estimated, giving $\beta = 0.76$ (0.04). Note the decrease in the standard error, which may occur because multicollinearity between $\log K_t$ and $\log L_t$ in the former version has been avoided by the transformation, so increasing the accuracy of the estimate. Under perfect competition (and omitting the error term) the marginal productivity condition gives $\beta = wL/pQ$, and the arithmetic mean labour share for the years 1909-1918 is calculated as 0.74. This correspondence apparently verifies marginal productivity theory as well as the Cobb-Douglas function. But wait!

Suppose again that the accounting convention $p_t Q_t = r_t K_t + w_t L_t$ holds in all periods, and that prices move in step, so that the price ratios $r/p$ and $w/p$ are constant over time. Then the data satisfy the equation

$$Q_t = \frac{r}{p} K_t + \frac{w}{p} L_t.$$

We can then show that the regression equation estimated by Douglas and his co-workers is a close approximation to this identity in the data, and there is little point in attempting to rediscover it. If all revenue is paid to either capital or labour it is difficult to distinguish between this accounting identity and the estimated equation.

To see this correspondence we need a linear approximation to the estimated equation. Using bars to denote arithmetic means, the regression equation can first be written in mean deviation form as

$$\log Q_t - \overline{\log Q} = \alpha(\log K_t - \overline{\log K}) + \beta(\log L_t - \overline{\log L}) + u_t - \overline{u}.$$

Now denoting the sample geometric means of the variables by $\tilde{Q}, \tilde{K}$ and $\tilde{L}$ respectively, we have $\log \tilde{Q} = \overline{\log Q}$, etc., and the estimated equation can be written

$$\log \frac{Q_t}{\tilde{Q}} = \alpha \log \frac{K_t}{\tilde{K}} + \beta \log \frac{L_t}{\tilde{L}} + e_t,$$

where $e_t$ is the regression residual. Now

$$\log \frac{Q_t}{\tilde{Q}} = \log \left( 1 + \frac{Q_t - \tilde{Q}}{\tilde{Q}} \right) \simeq \frac{Q_t - \tilde{Q}}{\tilde{Q}} = \frac{Q_t}{\tilde{Q}} - 1$$

using the approximation $\log(1+x) \doteq x$, and similarly for the other variables, so the estimated log-linear equation can be approximated by the linear relationship

$$\frac{Q_t}{\tilde{Q}} - 1 \simeq \hat{\alpha}\left( \frac{K_t}{\tilde{K}} - 1 \right) + \hat{\beta}\left( \frac{L_t}{\tilde{L}} - 1 \right),$$

that is,

$$Q_t \simeq \hat{\alpha} \frac{\bar{Q}}{\bar{K}} K_t + \hat{\beta} \frac{\bar{Q}}{\bar{L}} L_t + (1 - \hat{\alpha} - \hat{\beta}) \bar{Q}.$$

Comparing the coefficients of this equation with those of the accounting identity, we expect to find

$$\hat{\alpha} \frac{\bar{Q}}{\bar{K}} \simeq \frac{r}{p}, \hat{\beta} \frac{\bar{Q}}{\bar{L}} \simeq \frac{w}{p}, 1 - \hat{\alpha} - \hat{\beta} \sim 0.$$

Thus the regression coefficients $\alpha$ and $\beta$ correspond closely to factor shares and tend to exhibit constant returns to scale since the estimating equation is a close approximation to the accounting identity. So perhaps these Cobb-Douglas results and the apparent support for constant returns or marginal productivity theory are not as persuasive as was first supposed.

## TECHNICAL CHANGE

Time series estimation of a production function with fixed coefficients and assuming input homogeneity ignores any influences that technical change might have. The problem in time series studies of technical change is to distinguish movements along a production function, due to factor proportions changing over time, from shifts of the function, assumed due to technical progress. We consider *disembodied* technical progress, which arrives as "manna from heaven" with benefits freely available. The resulting shifts of the production function can be represented by including a time variable,

$$Q_t = F(K_t, L_t, t),$$

thus implying that the same input quantities yield a different output at different points of time. An alternative approach assumes that technical progress is *embodied* in capital or labour, thus the firm must invest in new capital goods or labour to gain its benefits. Advances are embodied in capital goods of different vintages, new machines being more productive than old machines, thus capital is no longer assumed homogeneous.

A *neutral* disembodied technical change (in Hicks' definition) is one which neither saves nor uses either factor, and so leaves the marginal rate of substitution unaltered. Technical change shifts the isoquants inwards, and Hicks-neutral technical change leaves the slope of the isoquants along a ray through the origin unchanged, thus there is no incentive to vary factor proportions unless relative factor prices change. If on the other hand the production function shifts so that (say) the marginal product of capital rises relative to that of labour for each factor combination – i.e. the marginal rate of substitution of $K$ for $L$ falls – then technical change is capital-using (labour-saving) and *non-neutral*.

In the Cobb-Douglas case the easiest way to incorporate neutral technical progress is to allow the scale parameter $A$ to vary, for this will not affect the marginal rate of substitution:

$$Q_t = A(t)K_t^\alpha L_t^\beta .$$

An early attempt by Tinbergen in this framework used the form $A(t) = A_0 e^{\lambda t}$, which is equivalent to introducing a trend term into the log-linear regression, but the problems of identification remain. The only way to obtain non-neutral change with the Cobb-Douglas function is to allow the ratio $\alpha/\beta$ to vary: if $\alpha$ rises relative to $\beta$ then technical change is capital-using, and vice versa. In general, variation in the elasticity of substitution would also result in non-neutral technical change, but the Cobb-Douglas function has a constant elasticity of one.

Solow (1957) sidesteps the identification problem in the context of constant returns by abandoning the Cobb-Douglas specification and making use of marginal productivity conditions in an attempt to differentiate shifts of from movements along the production function. Assuming that technical progress is neutral and disembodied (an untested hypothesis in Solow's work), we have

$$Q_t = A(t) F(K_t, L_t).$$

Differentiating with respect to time and denoting the derivatives by putting a dot over the variable, hence $dQ/dt = \dot{Q}$, we have

$$\dot{Q} = \dot{A}\, F(K_t, L_t) + A\frac{\partial F}{\partial K}\,\dot{K} + A\,\frac{\partial F}{\partial L}\,\dot{L}.$$

Dividing by $Q$ gives an equation for the proportionate rate of change of output:

$$\frac{\dot{Q}}{Q} = \frac{\dot{A}F(K_t, L_t)}{Q} + A\frac{\partial F}{\partial K}\frac{\dot{K}}{Q} + A\frac{\partial F}{\partial L}\frac{\dot{L}}{Q}.$$

Now we add the assumption that factors are paid their marginal products:

$$\frac{\partial Q}{\partial K} = A\frac{\partial F}{\partial K} = \frac{r}{p},\; \frac{\partial Q}{\partial L} = A\frac{\partial F}{\partial L} = \frac{w}{p}.$$

In Solow's notation the shares of capital and labour are denoted respectively by $w_K = rK/pQ$ and $w_L = wL/pQ$, thus with this assumption the preceding equation becomes

$$\frac{\dot{Q}}{Q} = \frac{\dot{A}}{A} + w_K\frac{\dot{K}}{K} + w_L\frac{\dot{L}}{L}.$$

Assuming constant returns to scale gives $w_L + w_K = 1$ by Euler's theorem and we can convert to *per capita* variables $q = K/L$ and $k = K/L$. The proportionate rates of change of the *per capita* variables are expressed in terms of the proportionate rates of change of the total volume variables as follows

$$\dot{q} = \frac{\dot{Q}}{L} - \frac{Q}{L^2}\,\dot{L},$$

and so

$$\frac{\dot{q}}{q} = \frac{\dot{Q}}{Q} - \frac{\dot{L}}{L},\; \frac{\dot{k}}{k} = \frac{\dot{K}}{K} - \frac{\dot{L}}{L}.$$

Substituting in, and using $w_L = 1 - w_K$, we have

$$\frac{\dot{q}}{q} = \frac{\dot{A}}{A} + w_K \frac{\dot{k}}{k} .$$

Approximating the continuous time derivatives by first differences in annual data, and given such data on output per man-hour, capital per man-hour and the share of capital, the technical change index $\Delta A(t)/A(t-1)$ can be calculated year by year from this relation. The results of this calculation then permit a series for $A(t)$ to be constructed by assuming an arbitrary initial value $A(1) = 1$ and repeatedly using the relation

$$A(t) = A(t-1) \left[ 1 + \frac{\Delta A(t)}{A(t-1)} \right], t=2, 3, \ldots .$$

The resulting series has a strong upward trend; the average rate of technical progress in the U.S. over the period 1909-1949 was 1.5% per annum.

Having got an estimate of how much the production function was shifting, Solow then asked how much of the increase in output per man-hour during the forty years was due to technical change (I in Figure 10), and how much was due to the increase in $k$ (II). An idea of

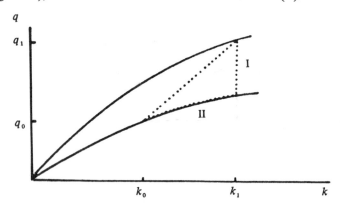

*Figure 10*

the fixed function corrected foɪ technical progress can be obtained by dividing $q(t)$ by $A(t)$. This estimates what would have occurred without technical change, that is the increase in output per man-hour attributable to the increase in capital. Solow found that technical change over the sample period accounted for 90% of the improvement in output per man-hour, and growth of capital the remaining 10%. As Solow acknowledged, his measure is a catch-all, incorporating any kind of shift in the production function – "slowdowns, speedups, improvements in the education of the labour force" (an embodied technical change) all appear as "technical change". A further difficulty with an aggregate measure such as this is that it ignores changes in the composition of output. For example if the economy utilises more intensively sectors which enjoy comparative advantages, but there is no technical progress, nevertheless the overall productivity measure will increase.

When $q/A$ is plotted against the capital-labour ratio as an indication of the underlying production function corrected for technical change, the Cobb-Douglas form $\log (q/A)$ on $\log k$ does as well as anything else. This is not too surprising since the Cobb-Douglas function would fit perfectly if factor shares were constant, and in fact they show little variability. (Solow spent some time in his original paper attempting to explain the 1943-1949 observations, which did not lie on the general relation between $q/A$ and $k$ given by the other observations. It turns out that these were the result of a computational error; see, for example, Hogan (1958) or the footnote to this effect on p.330 of the Solow paper as reprinted in Mueller (1969).)

## THE CES PRODUCTION FUNCTION

Neoclassical economics emphasises the substitutability between factors of production, the ease of which is measured by the elasticity parameter, $\sigma$. The Cobb-Douglas function constrains $\sigma$ to equal one, which may or may not be a good approximation. The constant elasticity of substitution (CES) production function also constrains the value of $\sigma$ to be constant, in the sense that it does not change with changes in relative prices or factor inputs. Its value is determined by the underlying technology and may change with technical progress, but in any event is not necessarily equal to one.

In the Cobb-Douglas case, under competitive conditions, the labour marginal productivity equation can be written, *since* $Q_L = \beta Q/L = \frac{w}{p}$

$$\log (Q/L) = - \log \beta + \log (w/p),$$

and so output per head varies with the real wage rate (logarithmically) with a coefficient of unity. In contrast, Arrow, Chenery, Minhas, and Solow (1961) — referred to as SMAC — observed cross-section regressions with a coefficient not equal to one,

$$\log (Q/L) = a + b \log (w/p),$$

and derived the CES production function as a solution to this equation. The function is

$$Q = \gamma \left\{ \delta K^{-\rho} + (1-\delta)L^{-\rho} \right\}^{-\nu/\rho}.$$

Writing the right-hand side as $F(K,L)$, then $F(hK,hL) = h^\nu F(K,L)$ and $\nu$ gives the degree of homogeneity: in the original SMAC study $\nu$ was taken equal to one and so constant returns were imposed, although the independent derivation by Brown and de Cani (1963) permits any degree of returns to scale. The parameter $\gamma$ is a scale parameter which can be used to denote efficiency: a shift in $\gamma$ is an example of neutral technical change. The degree to which technology is capital intensive is indicated by $\delta$, and when the production function is embedded in a particular economic model $\delta$ can be interpreted as the distribution parameter. The substitution parameter $\rho$ is equal to $(1-\sigma)/\sigma$ as we shall see. Rewriting the production function as

$$Q^{-\rho/\nu} = \gamma^{-\rho/\nu} \left\{ \delta K^{-\rho} + (1-\delta)L^{-\rho} \right\}$$

and differentiating with respect to $K$ and $L$ we have

$$-\frac{\rho}{\nu} Q^{-1-\rho/\nu} \frac{\partial Q}{\partial K} = - \rho\gamma^{-\rho/\nu} \delta K^{-\rho-1}$$

and

$$-\frac{\rho}{\nu} Q^{-1-\rho/\nu} \frac{\partial Q}{\partial L} = -\rho\gamma^{-\rho/\nu} (1-\delta)L^{-\rho-1} .$$

Therefore the marginal products of capital and labour are

$$\frac{\partial Q}{\partial K} = \nu\delta\gamma^{-\rho/\nu} \frac{Q^{1+\rho/\nu}}{K^{1+\rho}}, \quad \frac{\partial Q}{\partial L} = \nu(1-\delta)\gamma^{-\rho/\nu} \frac{Q^{1+\rho/\nu}}{L^{1+\rho}}$$

and the marginal rate of substitution is given as

$$R = \frac{\partial Q}{\partial L} \bigg/ \frac{\partial Q}{\partial K} = \frac{1-\delta}{\delta} \left(\frac{K}{L}\right)^{1+\rho}.$$

Taking logarithms in this relation we have

$$\log R = \log \frac{1-\delta}{\delta} + (1+\rho) \log \frac{K}{L}$$

and so the elasticity of substitution is equal to

$$\sigma = \frac{\mathrm{d} \log (K/L)}{\mathrm{d} \log R} = \frac{1}{1+\rho} .$$

(It can be shown that the CES production function reduces to the Cobb-Douglas as $\sigma \to 1$, i.e. as $\rho \to 0$.)

A major problem with the CES production function is that unlike the Cobb-Douglas, we cannot transform it into a linear-in-parameters form by operations such as taking logarithms. There is no method of linearising that will sort out the parameters and variables to give a directly estimable exact representation. Linear approximations have been used, alternatively estimation has proceeded via side relations such as marginal productivity conditions or factor share equations which result from adding standard economic assumptions to the CES specification. Nor is the cost function much help in this case. Following the general procedure described on p.45 we first equate the marginal rate of substitution to the factor price ratio:

$$\frac{F_L}{F_K} = \frac{1-\delta}{\delta} \left(\frac{K}{L}\right)^{1+\rho} = \frac{w}{r} \, .$$

This yields the relation

$$L = K \left[\frac{1-\delta}{\delta} \frac{r}{w}\right]^{\sigma}$$

which can be substituted in the production function

$$\left(\frac{Q}{\gamma}\right)^{-\rho/\nu} = \delta K^{-\rho} + (1-\delta)L^{-\rho}$$

$$= K^{-\rho} \left\{\delta + (1-\delta)^{\sigma}\delta^{\rho\sigma} \left(\frac{r}{w}\right)^{-\rho\sigma}\right\},$$

so that the cost-minimising level of capital input is given as

$$K = \left(\frac{Q}{\gamma}\right)^{1/\nu} \left\{\delta + (1-\delta)^{\sigma} \, \delta^{\rho\sigma} \left(\frac{r}{w}\right)^{-\rho\sigma}\right\}^{1/\rho}$$

$$= \left(\frac{Q}{\gamma}\right)^{1/\nu} r^{-\sigma} \delta^{\sigma}\left\{\delta^{\sigma} r^{1-\sigma} + (1-\delta)^{\sigma} w^{1-\sigma}\right\}^{1/\rho}$$

since $\sigma + (\sigma/\rho) = 1/\rho$.

Similarly for labour input we obtain

$$L = \left(\frac{Q}{\gamma}\right)^{1/\nu} w^{-\sigma} (1-\delta)^{\sigma}\left\{\delta^{\sigma} r^{1-\sigma} + (1-\delta)^{\sigma} w^{1-\sigma}\right\}^{1/\rho},$$

hence the cost function is

$$TC = rK + wL$$

$$= \left(\frac{Q}{\gamma}\right)^{1/\nu} \left\{\delta^{\sigma} r^{1-\sigma} + (1-\delta)^{\sigma} w^{1-\sigma}\right\}^{1/1-\sigma}$$

since $1 + (1/\rho) = 1/(1-\sigma)$. Again this cannot be expressed in a linear-in-parameters fashion, and so even in the economic context in which Nerlove estimated a Cobb-Douglas cost function, direct estimation of the CES parameters is not possible: it is necessary to follow less direct routes.

## ESTIMATION OF THE ELASTICITY OF SUBSTITUTION

Under appropriate assumptions such that the labour productivity condition $\partial Q/\partial L = w/p$ is satisfied, in the constant returns case ($\nu=1$) we have

$$(1-\delta)\gamma^{-\rho}\left(\frac{Q}{L}\right)^{1+\rho} = \frac{w}{p}.$$

Thus

$$(1-\delta)\gamma^{-\rho} = \frac{w}{p}\left(\frac{L}{Q}\right)^{1+\rho} \text{ or } \left\{(1-\delta)\gamma^{-\rho}\right\}^{1/1+\rho} = \left(\frac{wL}{pQ}\right)\left(\frac{w}{p}\right)^{\sigma-1}$$

and

$$\log\frac{wL}{pQ} = \sigma\log(1-\delta) + (1-\sigma)\log\frac{w}{p} + (\sigma-1)\log\gamma.$$

If $\sigma=1$ as in the Cobb-Douglas case, then labour's share is independent of both the wage rate and neutral technical progress. If $\sigma < 1$, labour's share rises if real wages increase faster than technical progress. Using this as a time series equation let neutral technical progress occur via changes in the parameter $\gamma$, i.e. $\gamma_t = \gamma_0 e^{\lambda t}$, where $\lambda$ is some constant rate. Then $\log\gamma_t = \log\gamma_0 + \lambda t$ and

$$\log\left(\frac{wL}{pQ}\right)_t = \left\{\sigma\log(1-\delta) + (\sigma-1)\log\gamma_0\right\} + (1-\sigma)\log\left(\frac{w}{p}\right)_t + (\sigma-1)\lambda t$$

so a trend variable appears in the share of labour relation. This was estimated by SMAC from Solow's time series technical progress data, with the following results:

$$(1-\hat{\sigma}) = 0.431, (\hat{\sigma}-1)\hat{\lambda} = -.003,$$

hence

$$\hat{\sigma} = 0.569, \hat{\lambda} = 0.008.$$

This provides evidence against the hypothesis that $\sigma=1$, and provides an estimate of technical progress at a rate of 1.8% per annum.[1]

In their cross-section study, not having data on capital or rate of return, SMAC estimated a further side relation derived from the labour marginal productivity condition:

$$\frac{Q}{L} = \left\{(1-\delta)\gamma^{-\rho}\right\}^{-1/1+\rho} \left(\frac{w}{p}\right)^{1/1+\rho},$$

thus

$$\log{(Q/L)} = -\sigma \log\left\{(1-\delta)\gamma^{-\rho}\right\} + \sigma \log{(w/p)},$$

so a 1% increase in real wages is associated with a $\sigma$% increase in average labour productivity. In fact this was the first SMAC regression equation referred to above (p.68), and we now see that $b$, the coefficient of log $(w/p)$, provides an estimate of $\sigma$. The equation was estimated for each of 24 industries from a cross-section of up to 19 countries, such a cross-section ensuring price variation in the sample. Of the 24 values of $\hat{\sigma}$ all but one were less than 1 (and the exceptional value of 1.011 was not significantly different from 1). Ten were significantly different

---

[1] To obtain this estimate note that SMAC use common logarithms, to the base 10, rather than the natural logarithms used elsewhere in this book. Thus strictly speaking, the expression for $\gamma_t$ should read $\gamma_0(10)^{\lambda t}$, and the estimate of 1.8% follows since $\log_{10}1.018 = 0.008$.

from 1 at the 5% level or better and four more at the 10% level. It was therefore claimed that $\sigma \neq 1$ and the CES function should be preferred to the Cobb-Douglas.

However, suppose that there are non-constant returns so that the labour marginal productivity condition becomes

$$\frac{\partial Q}{\partial L} = \nu(1-\delta)\gamma^{-\rho/\nu}\left(\frac{Q}{L}\right)^{1+\rho} Q^{-\rho+\rho/\nu} = \frac{w}{p}.$$

The regression equation is then

$$\log\frac{Q}{L} = \text{constant} + \sigma \log\frac{w}{p} + \rho\sigma(1 - \frac{1}{\nu}) \log Q.$$

There is no estimation of returns to scale in the original SMAC paper; $\nu = 1$ is assumed, equivalent to setting the last coefficient in this regression equal to zero. However, $\log Q$ appears among the regressors if $\nu \neq 1$, a possibility that should perhaps be investigated.

Questions that arise in any empirical study are whether the same model describes the generation of all sample observations or, on the other hand, are there structural breaks, and whether the data themselves reflect the appropriate economic magnitudes equally well across the sample, this latter question being particularly relevant to international cross-section studies. The price variation exhibited by the SMAC data is considerable, the unweighted across-industry average wage (1954) ranging from $3,841 in the U.S. to $213 in Iraq. Fuchs (1963) therefore divides the countries into two groups — more and less developed — and estimates for each separately. Again assuming constant returns he shows that the intercept term differs significantly between the two groups but the slope coefficient does not. In all but three of the 24 cases the estimated elasticity of substitution is greater than that obtained by SMAC, and it is significantly different from one in *only two* cases. However, the intercept term is smaller for the more developed countries, whereas one might expect it to be greater on the grounds that the more developed countries either are more efficient (they have a higher value-added per head for a given wage rate, that is, a higher value of $\gamma$) or employ a more capital-intensive technology (they have a higher value of δ). Fuchs explains this by the suggestion that observed wages in less developed economies fail to reflect labour costs fully. His argument is illustrated in Figure 11. The true relationship lies

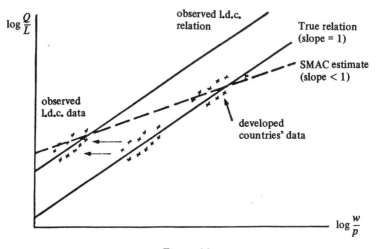

*Figure 11*

along a line with a slope of 1. But the under-recording of labour costs in less developed countries shifts observations on them to the left. The less developed countries will then be found to have a higher intercept term, but the slopes for developed and less developed countries will be the same. The SMAC estimate was based on data for both types of economy and so has a lower slope and higher intercept than the true (presumably Cobb-Douglas) relationship.

An alternative argument which achieves the same result is that the left-hand solid line is the "true" relation and the developed countries' observations are shifted to the right by virtue of trade union pressure, which achieves a higher real wage for given productivity than would be the case in less developed countries with less trade union activity.

A further example of a side relation permitting the estimation of the elasticity of substitution is provided by equating the marginal rate of substitution to the factor price ratio. Irrespective of the degree of returns to scale, we have

$$\frac{F_L}{F_K} = \frac{1-\delta}{\delta} \left(\frac{K}{L}\right)^{1+\rho} = \frac{w}{r}$$

hence

$$\log \frac{K}{L} = \sigma \log \frac{\delta}{1-\delta} + \sigma \log \frac{w}{r},$$

which can be estimated from data on the capital-labour ratio and relative factor prices, say time series data for a particular firm subject to changing demand, or cross-section data as in Nerlove's electricity supply study. In this regression an estimate of $\delta$ can be obtained from the intercept term. Note that $\delta$ is not invariant to units of measurement (though $\sigma$ is) and so cannot be readily compared between different studies. It can be standardised by using relative changes of variables or by converting data to index number form, the latter procedure also having the advantage of standardising the capital-labour ratio.

The problems of formulating appropriate economic and statistical models to allow consistent estimation of parameters of interest are no different in the CES case from those described previously. The regression equations discussed in this section are based on the first-order conditions for cost minimisation or profit maximisation, so it is assumed that the problem is set in an appropriate economic environment, that the disturbance terms reflect economic efficiency and that the regressors exhibit variation in the sample and are uncorrelated with the disturbances. Thus if the relevant prices are not given to the individual unit of observation but are affected by the unit's decisions via product or factor markets, then they cannot be treated as exogenous regressors. This is more likely to occur at a relatively high level of aggregation, such feedback being less likely at the firm than the industry level, individual firms being more likely to be price takers. Nerlove (1967) suggests the following possible scenarios: (i) all prices exogenous but varying from observation to observation; $Q$, $K$ and $L$ endogenous, (ii) $Q$ also exogenous, the firm minimising costs for given output, as in the study of regulated industries, (iii) $L$, $r$ and $p$ the three exogenous variables, as might be appropriate for inter-country comparisons when there is free trade, mobile capital, but immobile labour. The major finding of Nerlove's survey is "the diversity of results: even slight variations in the period or concepts tend to produce drastically different estimates of the elasticity" of substitution. In his comment on the paper Mansfield extends this conclusion to cover estimates of the rate of technical progress. Their discussion is mainly concerned with the biases which may or may not occur under various economic and statistical specifications and the difficulties which arise with various kinds of data: as we have seen, the specification problems are indeed considerable.

## ESTIMATION OF CES AND OTHER FUNCTIONAL FORMS

As noted initially, the CES production function is not readily translated into a simple linear form, and the early estimates of its parameters were obtained from linear regression equations based on first-order conditions as discussed in the previous section. We now discuss two subsequent developments.

First, direct estimation of the CES production function is now quite feasible by non-linear methods. To illustrate with the simplest case, we assume that the circumstances are such that the factor inputs are independent of the "technical efficiency" disturbance term, giving a least squares estimation problem. If the disturbance term is additive,

$$Q = \gamma \left\{ \delta K^{-\rho} + (1-\delta)L^{-\rho} \right\}^{-\nu/\rho} + u$$

then given a sample of $n$ observations on $Q$, $K$ and $L$ the residual sum of squares

$$\sum_{i=1}^{n} \left( Q_i - \gamma \left\{ \delta K_i^{-\rho} + (1-\delta)L_i^{-\rho} \right\}^{-\nu/\rho} \right)^2$$

is minimised with respect to $\gamma$, $\delta$, $\rho$ and $\nu$ by numerical methods. If the disturbance term is multiplicative, then the minimand is

$$\sum_{i=1}^{n} \ (\log Q_i - \log \gamma + \frac{\nu}{\rho} \log \left\{ \delta K_i^{-\rho} + (1-\delta) L_i^{-\rho} \right\})^2.$$

In either case algorithms exist to obtain estimates of the parameters and their approximate standard errors, see for example Mizon (1977).

Secondly, retracting a little, linear approximations to the CES function have been employed, and these have led to a further functional form, as we shall see. The approximation proposed by Kmenta (1967) is obtained by writing the CES function as

$$\log Q = \log \gamma - \frac{\nu}{\rho} f(\rho)$$

where $f(\rho) = \log \left\{ \delta K^{-\rho} + (1-\delta) L^{-\rho} \right\}$, and taking a Taylor series expansion of $f(\rho)$ around the value $\rho = 0$ (which corresponds to the value $\sigma = 1$). The general expansion is

$$f(\rho) - f(0) = \rho f'(0) + \tfrac{1}{2} \rho^2 f''(0) + \text{higher-order terms}$$

and the first and second derivatives evaluated at $\rho = 0$ are

$$f'(0) = -\left\{ \delta \log K + (1-\delta) \log L \right\}$$

$$f''(0) = \delta(1-\delta) \left\{ \log K - \log L \right\}^2,$$

so neglecting the higher-order terms we have the approximation

$$\log Q = \log \gamma + \nu\delta \log K + \nu(1-\delta) \log L - \tfrac{1}{2}\nu\rho\delta(1-\delta)\left\{ \log(K/L) \right\}^2.$$

In effect the squared logarithm of the capital-labour ratio is added to the Cobb-Douglas log-linear regression, and this last term indicates the departure from a unit elasticity of substitution. The regression coefficients yield estimates of the four parameters.

If, as suggested by Griliches and Ringstad (1971) and Sargan (1971), the squared term is replaced by an unconstrained quadratic, then we have the "transcendental logarithmic" (or "translog" for short) production function of Christensen *et al.* (1973), Berndt and Christensen (1973), etc.:

$$\log Q = a_0 + a_1 \log K + a_2 \log L + a_{11}(\log K)^2 + a_{12}(\log K)(\log L)$$

$$+ a_{22}(\log L)^2.$$

This is clearly a flexible general form that is easy to estimate and easy to specialise to less general forms. However in general output is not homogeneous in the inputs, and estimates of marginal products and the elasticity of substitution again require the calculation of functions of the coefficients. Moreover, marginal products are not necessarily positive and isoquants not necessarily convex at all combinations of input values, although this may not be a serious problem if the values of the input variables for which these conditions are not satisfied are extreme or atypical.

As discussed earlier in this chapter, in the accepted theoretical framework the production function expresses the *maximum* output obtainable from given factor inputs. However empirical studies based on statistical models incorporating random errors taking both positive and negative values (that is, having a two-sided distribution) in effect obtain estimates of *average* production functions. Following the work of Farrell (1957), there have been attempts to bring empirical studies closer to the theoretical framework by estimating *frontier* production functions. Thus if the maximum possible output obtainable by the $i$th firm, $i=1,\ldots,n$, from given inputs is written as

$$Q_i = F(K_i, L_i; \theta),$$

where $\theta$ is a vector of parameters, then one might seek a procedure to calculate an estimate $\hat{\theta}$ subject to the constraints

$$Q_i \leq F(K_i, L_i; \hat{\theta}), i=1,\ldots,n.$$

This suggests that the estimation procedure will become a mathematical programming problem, and if the function is linear in $\theta$ then choosing estimates to minimise

$$\sum_{i=1}^{n} |Q_i - F(K_i, L_i; \hat{\theta})| \text{ or } \sum_{i=1}^{n} \left\{ Q_i - F(K_i, L_i; \hat{\theta}) \right\}^2$$

subject to the constraints gives a linear or quadratic programming problem respectively. A statistical model that leads to these estimation procedures (Schmidt, 1976) is obtained by adding a disturbance term that has a one-sided distribution:

$$Q_i = F(K_i, L_i; \theta) + u_i, u_i \leq 0.$$

If $-u_i$ has an exponential or a half-normal distribution then maximum likelihood estimation of $\theta$ is equivalent to the above linear or quadratic programming procedure respectively. In practice these methods are extremely sensitive to outlying observations: whereas in a least-squares procedure an output observation somewhat greater than the central tendency would simply have a weight proportional to the squared discrepancy, in the present procedure it has a strong influence on the position of the frontier since all observations must lie on or inside the estimated frontier. If, on the other hand, some outliers are permitted to lie above the frontier, then this may be reconciled with the notion of the frontier as the maximum possible output by appealing to measurement error in the extreme observations. A model in which the random error term has two components, one a technical efficiency disturbance having a one-sided distribution and the other a measurement error having a symmetric distribution with mean zero, is presented by Aigner *et al.* (1977): this is termed a stochastic frontier production function model, and it represents an intermediate position between the average and frontier production function models.

Our aim in this chapter has been to illustrate general identification and specification problems in a particular area of application, and to indicate the difficulties that arise in empirically fleshing out the bare bones of this particular part of economic theory. Perhaps the sophistication of the statistical methods stands in sharp contrast to the simplicity of the concept of the production function. A survey of empirical results has not been our objective, nor has the aggregation problem received the attention it deserves in this and other contexts. Finally we have left on one side studies that are based on Johansen's (1959, 1972) reappraisal of the underlying notion of the production function, in which the traditional assumption of continuous substitution possibilities is replaced by the assumption that the firm's basic decision about factor proportions and the exploitation of new technologies is taken when investment in new plant and equipment occurs; subsequent decisions concern only the level of operation of the plant, current inputs being in fixed proportions to one another and to output. If such an approach is felt to be inapplicable to aggregate time series data except under very special circumstances, then perhaps as much is implied about the likely usefulness of an aggregate production function as about the relevance of the underlying model.

# III

# THE INVESTMENT FUNCTION

## INTRODUCTION: ACCELERATOR MODELS

The main work to be studied in this chapter is that of Jorgenson and his co-workers, whose theory of investment behaviour is "based on the neoclassical theory of optimal accumulation of capital". Here, in the tradition of Irving Fisher, the firm acts to maximise its net worth, defined as the present value of all future net cash flows. Before discussing Jorgenson's work, and then that of his critics, we first take a quick look at the more *ad hoc* tradition of investment studies, and then describe some generalisations of the simple geometric distributed lag function which have been applied in this field. Subsequently we consider models of interrelated factor demands.

A starting point is provided by the accelerator model, which assumes that there is a fixed capital-output ratio $\alpha$ so that net investment is given by

$$\Delta K_t = \alpha \Delta Q_t.$$

However this simple form gives very poor results, and the regression estimate of $\alpha$ typically does not correspond at all closely to a capital-output ratio estimate. The flexible accelerator (or stock adjustment hypothesis or partial adjustment hypothesis, using the terminology of chapter 1) provides a generalisation in which actual net investment is only a proportion of investment required to achieve the desired capital stock position, $K_t^*$. Thus

$$K_t - K_{t-1} = (1-\gamma)(K_t^* - K_{t-1}), \, 0 < \gamma < 1.$$

If it is assumed that the capital-output ratio determines the desired capital stock, then

$$K_t^* = \alpha Q_t$$

and

$$K_t = \alpha(1-\gamma)Q_t + \gamma K_{t-1}.$$

On repeated substitution for the lagged value this equation gives an expression for $K_t$ as a distributed lag function of $Q_t$ with geometrically declining coefficients

$$K_t = \alpha(1-\gamma)\Sigma\gamma^j Q_{t-j},$$

and it was in this context that the original Koyck work (1954) was undertaken. As we shall see, investment theories differ according to (a) the determinants of the firm's desired capital stock position, and (b) the specification of adjustment process. A third element, on which there is almost complete agreement, is that of replacement investment.

Gross investment $I_t$ is equal to net investment plus replacement investment $D_t$:

$$I_t = \Delta K_t + D_t;$$

alternatively, end-period capital stock equals beginning capital stock plus gross investment less depreciation:

$$K_t = K_{t-1} + I_t - D_t.$$

The standard assumption is that replacement demand or depreciation is proportional to the existing stock:

$$D_t = \delta K_{t-1},$$

thus

$$I_t = K_t - (1-\delta)K_{t-1}.$$

This together with the partial adjustment hypothesis yields the following equation for gross investment:

$$I_t = (1-\gamma)K_t^* - (1-\gamma-\delta)K_{t-1} \ .$$

Such models have been used to study not only investment in capital goods but also the demand for consumers' durable goods, when $I_t$ represents purchases during period $t$ and the desired stock depends on prices and consumers' income. For example, the studies in Harberger (1960), dealing with housing, refrigerators, automobiles, farm tractors, and corporate investment, are all of this type. When an expression for $K_t^*$ is substituted into this equation, whether it is of the simple form $\alpha Q_t$ or includes a number of determinants of the desired stock, the parameters are not identified, since the number of regression coefficients (equal to the number of determinants of $K_t^*$ plus one) is one less than the number of parameters. This difficulty might be overcome by obtaining an extraneous estimate of $\delta$, for example from data on prices of new and second-hand goods or from information about the practice of accountants or tax assessors in calculating depreciation. Alternatively the equation can be transformed to eliminate $K_{t-1}$, which is also useful if stock data are unavailable or unreliable (as is usually the case):

$$I_t - (1-\delta)I_{t-1} = (1-\gamma)\left\{K_t^* - (1-\delta)K_{t-1}^*\right\}$$
$$- (1-\gamma-\delta)\left\{K_{t-1} - (1-\delta)K_{t-2}\right\}$$
$$= (1-\gamma)\left\{K_t^* - (1-\delta)K_{t-1}^*\right\} - (1-\gamma-\delta)I_{t-1},$$

and so

$$I_t = (1-\gamma)K_t^* - (1-\gamma)(1-\delta)K_{t-1}^* + \gamma I_{t-1} \ .$$

In the simple case in which $K_t^* = \alpha Q_t$, a regression of $I_t$ on $Q_t$, $Q_{t-1}$ and $I_{t-1}$ yields estimates of $\alpha$, $\gamma$ and $\delta$. However, if $K_t^*$ depends on two or more variables, say price $P_t$ and income $Y_t$ in the case of consumer durables, then the underlying parameters are now overidentified. Writing

$$K_t^* = \alpha_1 P_t + \alpha_2 Y_t ,$$

the regression equation has five coefficients (of $P_t$, $Y_t$, $P_{t-1}$, $Y_{t-1}$ and $I_{t-1}$) which are functions of four parameters ($\alpha_1$, $\alpha_2$, $\gamma$ and $\delta$), and so unique parameter estimates cannot be deduced. This difficulty can be overcome by choosing a number of values of $\delta$, then for each value constructing the series

$$P_t^\dagger = P_t - (1-\delta)P_{t-1} , \; Y_t^\dagger = Y_t - (1-\delta) Y_{t-1}$$

and estimating the regression

$$I_t = \alpha_1(1-\gamma)P_t^\dagger + \alpha_2(1-\gamma) Y_t^\dagger + \gamma I_{t-1} ,$$

and finally selecting that value of $\delta$ which minimises the residual sum of squares. Estimates of $\alpha_1$, $\alpha_2$, and $\gamma$ are then derived from the regression coefficients obtained with this value of $\delta$. This method is in effect a non-linear least squares algorithm, and it was suggested by Nerlove (1960) in the context of the study of expenditure on consumer durables by Stone and Rowe (1960).

Returning to the context of investment in physical capital, there are two main groups of variables which have been considered as relevant determinants of $K^*$. The use of output or sales in an accelerator framework has already been mentioned. Possible extensions are the use of expected or forecast sales in place of actual sales, the averaging of sales to eliminate short-run fluctuations, and corrections for the under-utilisation of capacity on the assumption that there is a fixed relation between $K^*$ and *potential* output. The second group of determinants of $K^*$ are financial variables, such as current or past levels of profits and the rate of return. Profits are relevant on the argument that investment is constrained by the supply of internal funds. The question of what variables influence the level of investment is of importance for maintaining stability, promoting growth, and so forth, and the policy implications of the two groups of variables are different. For example if investment is a function of profits, then corporate taxes will be an important policy instrument. On the other hand, if investment depends on sales or demand expectations, corporate taxes will have little effect, and more appropriate instruments would be purchase taxes and demand stimulants. In practice, the justifications for either approach have been rather intuitive and rough-and-ready, and Jorgenson's model represented an important development, relating investment behaviour to profit maximising considerations. As a preliminary, we next discuss generalisations of the simple partial adjustment process.

## DISTRIBUTED LAG FUNCTIONS

The general distributed lag model determining the variable $y$ as a function of current and past values of the variable $x$, together with an error term, is

$$y_t = \sum_{j=0}^{\infty} \mu_j x_{t-j} + u_t.$$

The $\mu$-coefficients are sometimes termed reaction coefficients, since a unit impulse in the $x$-series causes a reaction $\mu_j$ in the $y$-series with a lag of $j$ periods. If the change in $x$ is a unit step, that is, a maintained increase in the level of the series, then the response of $y$ over time is described by the partial sums of the $\mu$'s, and the total or long-run multiplier, giving the change in the equilibrium value of $y$ in response to a unit increase in $x$, is equal to the complete sum

$$\sum_{0}^{\infty} \mu_j.$$

Of course this general distributed lag function, containing an infinite number of coefficients, is simply a mathematically convenient general form and has no empirical usefulness without further assumptions. Such assumptions express the reaction coefficients in terms of a small number of parameters, but since economic theory typically offers little guidance about the time form of the response of one variable to

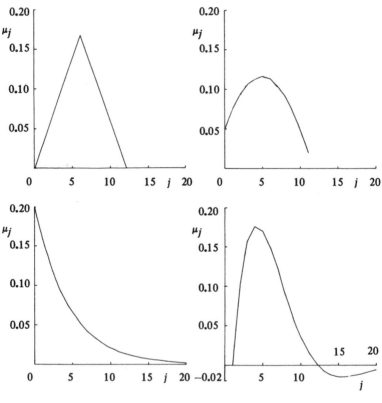

*Figure 12*

changes in another, it is important in practice to avoid para-
meterisations that are unduly restrictive, unless of course a restricted
form has been demonstrated to fit the data as well as a more general
form. Four of the distributed lag functions that we discuss below are
illustrated in Figure 12. Since we are working in discrete time, strictly
speaking these should be sketched as bar charts, but a continuous line
often brings out the shape more effectively, and in one case the
parameterisation is obtained in terms of an expression for this
continuous function, as we shall see. In each of the four cases the
long-run multiplier is equal to one.

A first possibility is to postulate a maximum lag of $m$ periods, say, after which there is no further response in $y$ to the change in $x$. Thus

$$\mu_{m+1} = \mu_{m+2} = \ldots = 0,$$

and

$$y_t = \sum_{j=0}^{m} \mu_j x_{t-j} + u_t.$$

In principle, there is no difficulty in directly estimating the $\mu$'s, provided that the number of observations is greater than $m$. If the error term is independent of $x$ and non-autocorrelated, then OLS will provide best, linear unbiased estimates. In practice, however, two difficulties are likely to arise. First, although $m$ must be less than the sample size, it might still need to be relatively large, and so leave relatively few degrees of freedom for the estimation process. Second, irrespective of the behaviour of the error term, the $x$-variable is itself likely to be autocorrelated, resulting in multicollinearity problems − in particular, estimates of the $\mu$'s will tend to have large standard errors, and the general shape of the lag response function will not be very well determined. Consequently further assumptions about the shape of the lag distribution are necessary, in order to represent the $m+1$ coefficients as functions of a smaller number of parameters.

De Leeuw (1962) applied the "inverted $V$" lag distribution in which the coefficients increase linearly from $\mu_0 = 0$ to a peak at a lag of $m/2$ periods (assuming $m$ even), and then decrease to zero at the same rate (this assumes $\mu_m = 0$). Thus, once the value of $m$ is specified, there remains only one parameter to be estimated, for the lag distribution is completely determined by $\mu_{m/2}$, the height of the peak. In practice, different values of $m$ were tried, and the value resulting in maximum $R^2$ chosen. (The case $m = 12$ is sketched in the top left panel of Figure 12.)

This approach is generalised by Almon (1965), who assumes that the lag distribution can be represented as a low-degree polynomial. Thus, writing the polynomial as

$$f(z) = \alpha_0 + \alpha_1 z + \alpha_2 z^2 + \ldots + \alpha_k z^k = \sum_{i=0}^{k} \alpha_i z^i,$$

the coefficients $\mu_0, \mu_1, \ldots, \mu_m$ are given by the values of $f(z)$ at the points $z = 0, 1, \ldots, m$, that is

$$\mu_j = \sum_{i=0}^{k} \alpha_i j^i.$$

The number of parameters required to specify the distribution is then $k+1$, chosen to be rather less than the number of coefficients $m+1$. Making the substitution $\mu_j = f(j)$, the model becomes

$$y_t = \sum_{j=0}^{m} \left( \sum_{i=0}^{k} \alpha_i j^i \right) x_{t-j} + u_t$$

$$= \sum_{i=0}^{k} \alpha_i \left( \sum_{j=0}^{m} j^i x_{t-j} \right) + u_t,$$

and so constructing new variables

$$x_{it} = \sum_{j=0}^{m} j^i x_{t-j},$$

the equation to be estimated is

$$y_t = \sum_{i=0}^{k} \alpha_i x_{it} + u_t.$$

In practice, the construction of the new variables and the calculation of the $m+1$ $\mu$-coefficients from the $k+1$ estimated $\alpha$'s is all carried out in widely-available computer packages. The degree of the polynomial, $k$, and the maximal lag, $m$, remain to be specified, so there is considerable scope for experimentation. Note that the polynomial $f(z)$ is only used in the range $0 \leq z \leq m$; outside this range the lag coefficients are specified to be zero, and the polynomial is not employed. However a further possibility, as applied by Almon, is to tie the lag distribution down by requiring the polynomial to give a zero value on either side, i.e. $f(-1) = f(m+1) = 0$ — these restrictions imply that only $k-1$ other parameters are required to specify the polynomial. But there is no particular reason to do this in general, and the evidence is that it tends to unnecessarily restrict the shape of the lag distribution; otherwise the range of possible shapes with a fourth-degree polynomial, as used by Almon, is quite wide. In estimating the distributed lag between capital appropriations and expenditures at the industry level, Almon's maximal lag varied between four and nine quarters. (The top right panel of Figure 12 gives an example with $k = 2$ and $m = 11$.)

After estimating either an inverted $V$ or a polynomial lag structure, the hypothesis that the lag structure is of this form can be tested, using the residual sum of squares, under the maintained hypothesis that the maximal lag is $m$ periods. This entails the computation of the residual sum of squares in an unrestricted multiple regression of $y_t$ on $x_t$, $x_{t-1}, \ldots, x_{t-m}$ (without necessarily paying any attention to the coefficients), and a comparison with that obtained subject to the polynomial restriction. If the polynomial lag structure has a significantly higher residual sum of squares, then the data reject the restriction, and the polynomial hypothesis cannot be accepted.

In a second group of distributed lag specifications a finite maximal lag is not assumed, but the coefficients approach zero asymptotically through various generalisations of the geometric lag structure. The simple geometric pattern is given by

$$y_t = \mu_0 x_t + \mu_0 \gamma x_{t-1} + \mu_0 \gamma^2 x_{t-2} + \mu_0 \gamma^3 x_{t-3} + \ldots + u_t,$$

$0 < \gamma < 1$, and this is illustrated in the lower left panel of Figure 12. In his investment studies, Koyck (1954) assumed that the geometric decline began after the second coefficient, so that

$$y_t = \mu_0 x_t + \mu_1 x_{t-1} + \mu_1 \gamma x_{t-2} + \mu_1 \gamma^2 x_{t-3} + \ldots + u_t$$

and three parameters are required. Evans (1967) introduced a double distributed lag to account for modifications to original investment plans, and the time response of net investment to an increase in sales has the shape of an inverted *W*. The first peak occurs at a lag of one quarter, the coefficients decline for three quarters, the second peak occurs at a six-quarter leg, then the geometric decline sets in. To discuss further generalisations, it is convenient to introduce lag operator notation.

The lag operator L is defined by

$$Lx_t = x_{t-1}$$

and with repeated application, we have

$$L^j x_t = x_{t-j} \, .$$

The advantage of this approach is that we can carry out algebraic operations with L as if it were an ordinary variable. Thus

$$L^j L^k = L^{j+k}$$

since both applied to $x_t$ give $x_{t-j-k}$, and if $\alpha_1$, $\alpha_2$ are constants, then

$$L^j(\alpha_1 x_{1t} + \alpha_2 x_{2t}) = \alpha_1 L^j x_{1t} + \alpha_2 L^j x_{2t} = \alpha_1 x_{1,t-j} + \alpha_2 x_{2,t-j}.$$

The general lag function can now be written

$$\Sigma \mu_j x_{t-j} = \Sigma \mu_j L^j x_t = \mu(L) x_t$$

where $\mu(L)$ is the infinite-degree polynomial in L

$$\mu(L) = \mu_0 + \mu_1 L + \mu_2 L^2 + \dots \, .$$

and the problem at hand is that of expressing $\mu(L)$, or approximating it, in terms of a finite number of parameters. Negative powers of the lag operator, and division by functions of it, can be readily interpreted. By $(1/L)x_t$ we mean that variable which yields $x_t$ when L is applied, namely $x_{t+1}$, and by $(1/\mu(L))y_t$ we mean that variable which results in $y_t$ when $\mu(L)$ is applied. Thus if

$$y_t = \mu(L)x_t \text{ then } \frac{1}{\mu(L)} y_t = x_t \, .$$

The Koyck transformation for the case of geometrically declining coefficients can be easily cast in this framework. We have

$$y_t = \mu_0 x_t + \mu_0 \gamma x_{t-1} + \mu_0 \gamma^2 x_{t-2} + \ldots + u_t$$

$$= \mu_0 (x_t + \gamma L x_t + \gamma^2 L^2 x_t + \ldots) + u_t$$

$$= \mu_0 (1 + \gamma L + \gamma^2 L^2 + \ldots) x_t + u_t$$

$$= \frac{\mu_0}{1-\gamma L} x_t + u_t$$

applying the formula for the sum of a geometric series. Thus in this simple case the lag polynomial $\mu(L)$ is given as $\mu_0/(1-\gamma L)$, and on multiplying through by $(1-\gamma L)$ we obtain

$$(1-\gamma L)y_t = \beta x_t + (1-\gamma L)u_t$$

that is, as before,

$$y_t = \gamma y_{t-1} + \beta x_t + (u_t - \gamma u_{t-1}).$$

Jorgenson (1963 *et seq.*) approximates the general infinite distributed lag function by a ratio of two finite-degree polynomials in L. It is assumed that

$$\mu(L) = \frac{\gamma(L)}{\omega(L)} = \frac{\gamma_0 + \gamma_1 L + \ldots + \gamma_k L^k}{\omega_0 + \omega_1 L + \ldots + \omega_l L^l},$$

and this is referred to as a *rational lag function*. Any lag function can be approximated by a rational lag function as closely as we like by making $k$ and/or $l$ sufficiently large, but the general objective is to keep them quite small. This generalises the schemes discussed so far: the Almon lag structure is obtained when $\omega(L) = 1$ and the numerator polynomial is suitably restricted, and the geometric lag structure has $k=0$ and $l=1$. The generalisation of the Koyck transformation is immediate, for if

$$y_t = \frac{\gamma(L)}{\omega(L)} x_t + u_t$$

then

$$\omega(L)y_t = \gamma(L)x_t + \omega(L)u_t.$$

(The conventional normalisation rule is to set $\omega_0 = 1$.) The estimating equation contains $l$ lagged values of the dependent variable and $k$ lagged values of the explanatory variable, and has an error term which is an $l$-order moving average of the original disturbance term. Thus if $u_t$ is independent, $\omega(L)u_t$ is autocorrelated, and OLS will provide inconsistent estimates, so alternative estimators may be required.

Finally, we illustrate the operations of multiplication and division of polynomials in L. The net effect of the successive application of two polynomials in L to a given series is evaluated by calculating their product or "convolution". If $\gamma(L)$ and $\omega(L)$ are of degree $k$ and $l$ respectively as above, then applying both to a given series will produce a maximum lag of $k+l$ periods, and their product $\alpha(L)$ is a polynomial in L of degree $k+l$:

$$\alpha(L)x_t = \gamma(L)\omega(L)x_t.$$

The two polynomials on either side of this equation are equivalent if the coefficients of each separate power of L correspond, so the $\alpha$-coefficients are obtained by picking out the coefficients of particular powers of L on the right-hand side. We have

$$(\alpha_0 + \alpha_1 L + \alpha_2 L^2 + \ldots + \alpha_{l+k} L^{l+k})$$
$$= (\gamma_0 + \gamma_1 L + \ldots + \gamma_k L^k)(\omega_0 + \omega_1 L + \ldots + \omega_l L^l)$$

and equating coefficients gives

$$
\begin{aligned}
\text{constant term:} \quad & \alpha_0 = \gamma_0 \omega_0 \\
\text{coefficient of L:} \quad & \alpha_1 = \gamma_0 \omega_1 + \gamma_1 \omega_0 \\
\text{coefficient of } L^2: \quad & \alpha_2 = \gamma_0 \omega_2 + \gamma_1 \omega_1 + \gamma_2 \omega_0 \\
& \vdots \\
\text{coefficient of } L^{l+k}: \quad & \alpha_{l+k} = \gamma_k \omega_l.
\end{aligned}
$$

Thus the joint effect of two or more polynomials in L can be easily calculated.

We consider division of polynomials in L by asking how the $\mu$-coefficients in the rational lag function $\mu(L) = \gamma(L)/\omega(L)$ can be calculated from the given polynomials $\gamma(L)$ and $\omega(L)$. One approach is to factorise $\omega(L)$ and so express $1/\omega(L)$ in partial fractions, and then obtain a power series expansion for each term separately. The ratio $\mu(L)$ is in general of infinite degree, although we require that $\mu_j \to 0$ as $j \to \infty$. The following illustration uses numbers similar to those obtained by Jorgenson, who typically took $l=2$, thus adding one extra lagged value of the dependent variable to the Koyck-transformed regression equation. Taking

$$
\omega(L) = (1 - 1.25\, L + .375\, L^2),
$$

the coefficients of the lagged dependent variables, when written on the right-hand side of the equation, are 1.25 and $-.375$. We require the reciprocal of this, expressed in terms of positive powers of L, so that we can interpret $(1/\omega(L))x_t$. First, $\omega(L)$ is factorised, giving

$$
\omega(L) = (1 - .75\, L)(1 - .5\, L).
$$

Then, applying the method of partial fractions, we write

$$
\frac{1}{\omega(L)} = \frac{1}{(1 - \tfrac{3}{4}L)(1 - \tfrac{1}{2}L)} = \frac{A}{1 - \tfrac{3}{4}L} + \frac{B}{1 - \tfrac{1}{2}L}
$$

and solve for $A$ and $B$ by comparing the numerators when the last expression is put over a common denominator. Thus

$$\frac{1}{(1-\tfrac{3}{4}L)(1-\tfrac{1}{2}L)} = \frac{A(1-\tfrac{1}{2}L)+B(1-\tfrac{3}{4}L)}{(1-\tfrac{3}{4}L)(1-\tfrac{1}{2}L)}$$

and the two sides are equivalent if the numerators match up. Since the numerator on the left contains a constant and no power of L, we require

$$1 = A + B \quad \text{and} \quad 0 = -\tfrac{1}{2}A - \tfrac{3}{4}B$$

hence $A = 3$ and $B = -2$, or

$$\frac{1}{\omega(L)} = \frac{3}{1-\tfrac{3}{4}L} - \frac{2}{1-\tfrac{1}{2}L} .$$

We can now express this as a power series in L by the usual binomial expansion, reversing the operation of summing a geometric series, that is,

$$\frac{1}{\omega(L)} = 3\left\{1 + \tfrac{3}{4}L + (\tfrac{3}{4}L)^2 + (\tfrac{3}{4}L)^3 + \ldots\right\}$$
$$- 2\left\{1 + \tfrac{1}{2}L + \tfrac{1}{4}L^2 + \tfrac{1}{8}L^3 + \ldots\right\}.$$

Calculating the first few coefficients gives

$$\frac{1}{\omega(L)} = 1 + 1.25\,L + 1.1875\,L^2 + 1.0156\,L^3$$
$$+ .8242\,L^4 + .6494\,L^5 + .5027\,L^6 + \ldots$$

We see that the coefficients are made up of increasing powers of $\tfrac{3}{4}$ and $\tfrac{1}{2}$, and so tend to zero. It is only when the coefficients of increasing powers of L do approach zero asymptotically that the reciprocal of the polynomial $\omega(L)$ has a well-defined meaning. The condition for this to hold is that when $\omega(L)$ is factorised, the coefficient of L in each factor should lie between $-1$ and $1$, as indeed they do in our example. The requirement that these coefficients are less than 1 in absolute value generalises the requirement that $|\gamma| < 1$ in first order, simple geometric models and ensures that the difference equation $\omega(L)y_t = a$ is stable. Lastly $\mu(L) = \gamma(L)/\omega(L)$ is obtained by multiplying this expression for $1/\omega(L)$ by $\gamma(L)$ using the method of the previous paragraph. Since $\gamma(L)$ is of finite degree and has finite coefficients, it will not affect these stability or convergence properties, so the condition on the factors of $\omega(L)$ is sufficient to ensure that $\mu_j \to 0$ as $j \to \infty$.

An alternative approach to calculating the coefficients in $\mu(L) = \gamma(L)/\omega(L)$ is to write down the relations between coefficients resulting from the equation $\gamma(L) = \omega(L)\mu(L)$, as follows ($\omega_0 = 1$):

$$\gamma_0 = \mu_0$$
$$\gamma_1 = \mu_0 \omega_1 + \mu_1$$
$$\gamma_2 = \mu_0 \omega_2 + \mu_1 \omega_1 + \mu_2$$

and so on, *ad infinitum*. Given the $\omega$'s and $\gamma$'s, these equations can then be solved recursively for the $\mu$'s. In the example sketched in the lower right panel of Figure 12, $\gamma(L)$ is of the simple form $\gamma_2 L^2$ which implies that $\mu_0 = \mu_1 = 0$, and $\omega(L)$ is of second degree, with complex conjugate roots.

Calculation of the long run multiplier implied by a rational lag function is straightforward. For the general lag polynomial $\mu(L)$ the long-run multiplier is $\Sigma\mu_j = \mu(1)$, that is, the polynomial is evaluated at 1. For the rational lag function $\mu(1) = \gamma(1)/\omega(1)$, and so we simply take the ratio of the sums of the $\gamma$- and $\omega$-coefficients. In our reciprocal polynomial example, the sum of the infinite series of coefficients, of which the first seven are given above, is $(1 - 1.25 + .375)^{-1} = 8$.

## NEOCLASSICAL MODELS

The accelerator models discussed initially rest on relatively little economic theory. We now discuss "neoclassical" models of investment behaviour, based on the theory of the firm's demand for capital as a factor of production (Jorgenson, 1963, 1965, 1967).

The firm is assumed to maximise net worth, that is, the present value of the stream of net revenues accruing to the firm over time. Net revenue at time $t$ is equal to income less outlay on current account less outlay on capital account:

$$R(t) = p(t)Q(t) - w(t)L(t) - q(t)I(t),$$

where $Q(t)$ is the amount of output and $p(t)$ its price, $L(t)$ is the amount of labour (or variable) input and $w(t)$ its price, $I(t)$ is the volume of gross investment and $q(t)$ the price of capital goods. Sales are equal to output, and there is no investment in stocks of finished goods. Output $Q(t)$ is the maximum that can be produced given capital stock $K(t)$ (associated capital services being assumed proportional to the stock) and labour services $L(t)$, and this is described by the production function

$$Q(t) = F\{K(t),L(t)\}$$

which is assumed to have the usual neoclassical properties and so admits factor substitutability. The relation between the capital stock $K(t)$ and the rate of investment $I(t)$ is given as

$$\dot{K}(t) = I(t) - \delta K(t),$$

where, again, a dot over a variable denotes the time derivative, $\dot{K}(t) = dK(t)/dt$, and the homogeneous capital stock decays at an exponential rate $\delta$. At time zero the present value of all future net revenues of the firm is

$$W = \int_0^\infty e^{-rt} R(t)dt,$$

where the market interest rate or discount rate $r$ is assumed constant for simplicity. The firm's problem is to choose a production plan to maximise net worth subject to the preceding two constraints, this production plan being given as a sequence of capital and labour inputs. All variables are continuous functions of time, thus there is no "lumpiness" of investment projects, this perfectly malleable capital can be bought and sold freely, and the firm is a price taker in all markets.

Finally in this simple model there are no adjustment costs or delivery delays.

The relevant Lagrangean function is

$$\mathcal{L} = \int_0^\infty \left[ e^{-rt} [p(t)F\{K(t),L(t)\} - w(t)L(t) - q(t)I(t)] \right. $$
$$\left. + \lambda(t)\{\dot{K}(t) - I(t) + \delta K(t)\} \right] dt. \quad = \int f \, dt$$

The production function constraint has been eliminated by substitution,[1] and the remaining Lagrange multiplier is written as a function of time since capital stock and investment must satisfy this relation at all times. The integrand is of the form $f(x,t,\dot{x})$, containing not only the variables with respect to which we are maximising, but also the time derivative of one of these variables. In this case it is not appropriate simply to maximise $f$ with respect to $x$ in every time period, since the rate of change variable causes links between different time periods. The appropriate procedure follows from Euler's equation, which is a slight generalisation of the standard first-order necessary condition. We require that the usual first partial derivative be equated not to zero but to the time derivative of the first partial derivative with respect to the rate of change variable, that is,

$$\frac{\partial f}{\partial x} = \frac{\mathrm{d}}{\mathrm{d}t}\left(\frac{\partial f}{\partial \dot{x}}\right)$$

(see for example Allen, 1938, ch.20). This does not present a problem when maximising with respect to $L(t)$ and $I(t)$, since their rates of change do not enter. Setting the first partial derivative with respect to $L(t)$ equal to zero leads to

$$p(t)\frac{\partial F\{K(t),L(t)\}}{\partial L} = w(t),$$

the usual marginal productivity condition for labour. Next we have

$$\frac{\partial f}{\partial I} = -e^{-rt}q(t) - \lambda(t) = 0.$$

[1] Jorgenson writes the production function in implicit form, that is, as $\mathcal{F}\{Q(t), K(t), L(t)\} = 0$, and enters this directly as a constraint with its own Lagrange multiplier.

Finally, making use of Euler's equation, we require

$$e^{-rt}p(t)\frac{\partial F\{K(t),L(t)\}}{\partial K} + \delta\lambda(t) = \frac{d\lambda(t)}{dt}. \qquad (a)$$

Differentiating the preceding equation with respect to time gives

$$\frac{d\lambda(t)}{dt} = e^{-rt}\{rq(t) - \dot{q}(t)\},$$

and on substituting for $\lambda(t)$ from the same equation and cancelling $e^{-rt}$ we obtain

$$p(t)\frac{\partial F\{K(t),L(t)\}}{\partial K} = (r+\delta)q(t) - \dot{q}(t).$$

The result is the marginal productivity condition for capital services, where the right-hand side, denoted $c(t)$, is the cost of using the services of one unit of capital stock for one time period.

Instead of relying on Euler's equation we can make a direct argument leading to this latter condition as follows. Consider the effects of planning at time zero to purchase an incremental unit of capital at time $\tau$. The net addition to the present value of the firm is then equal to

$$\int_\tau^\infty e^{-rt}\, e^{-\delta(t-\tau)}\, p(t)\frac{\partial F\{K(t),L(t)\}}{\partial K}\, dt - q(\tau)e^{-r\tau},$$

and the necessary condition for maximum present value is that this quantity is zero. That is, the marginal cost of the extra unit is equal to the total discounted future values of its marginal products. Since the contribution to $W$ of the incremental unit of capital must be zero irrespective of the time $\tau$ at which it is purchased, the derivative of this contribution with respect to $\tau$ is also zero. Thus

$$\delta\int_\tau^\infty e^{-rt}\, e^{-\delta(t-\tau)}\, p(t)\frac{\partial F(t)}{\partial K}\, dt - e^{-r\tau}p(\tau)\frac{\partial F(\tau)}{\partial K} - \dot{q}(\tau)e^{-r\tau}$$

$$+ rq(\tau)e^{-r\tau} = 0$$

for all $\tau$ and on substituting $q(\tau)e^{-r\tau}$ for the integral (from the previous expression) and cancelling out $e^{-r\tau}$ the marginal productivity condition is obtained (albeit with a change in the symbol denoting time).

The cost of capital $c(t) = (r+\delta)q(t) - \dot{q}(t)$ is termed "user cost" by Jorgenson, although as Tobin (1967) comments, in Keynes' terminology user cost is the "reduction in value of equipment due to using it as compared to not using it" and the fall in value of equipment depends on the intensity of use. These effects are absent in this model, where $c$ is an ownership or rental cost. As a simple discrete-time illustration, consider the cost of using one machine for one time period. Funds are borrowed to purchase the machine at a price of $q_t$, and the cost of these funds over the period is $rq_t$. At the end of the period only $(1-\delta)$ of the machine is left, which is sold at the prevailing price per unit, now $q_{t+1}$. So the total cost is $q_t + rq_t - (1-\delta)q_{t+1}$, i.e. $c \simeq q(r+\delta) - \Delta q$, equal to the cost of funds plus depreciation less capital gains.

Taxation is often introduced into the model, permitting the study of the effect on investment of changing tax parameters, by redefining net worth as the present value of revenue net of taxes:

$$W = \int_0^\infty e^{-rt} \left\{ R(t) - T(t) \right\} \mathrm{d}t.$$

Of course a tax on pure profits does not alter the profit-maximising levels of output and inputs, but in practice taxes are levied on "taxable" profits which differ from pure profits because, for example, special investment allowances may affect the definition of depreciation for tax purposes, or capital gains may not be fully taxed. It is assumed that income tax is charged at some rate $u$ $(0 \leq u \leq 1)$ on gross income less outlay on current account and certain capital allowances. Let $v_1$ be the proportion of depreciation $q\delta K$ deductible, $v_2$ be the proportion of interest payments $rqK$ deductible, and $v_3$ be the proportion of capital gains $\dot{q}K$ subject to tax. Then the tax function, deleting the time variable for convenience, is

$$T(t) = u\left\{ pQ - wL - v_1 q\delta K - v_2 rqK + v_3 \dot{q}K \right\}$$

$$= u[pQ - wL - \left\{ q(v_1\delta + v_2 r) - v_3\dot{q} \right\}K].$$

The effect of introducing this is to convert $c$ into an "after tax" cost:

$$c = q\left\{ \left(\frac{1-uv_1}{1-u}\right) \delta + \left(\frac{1-uv_2}{1-u}\right) r\right\} - \left(\frac{1-uv_3}{1-u}\right) \dot{q} \; .$$

Each of the factors $(1-uv_i)/(1-u)$ is greater than 1 unless $v_i = 1$, but in this latter case the introduction of taxation has no effect: the cost of capital is unchanged as $u$ varies if all tax allowances are correct, as noted above. Otherwise $c$ is increased unless all depreciation and interest is tax deductible, and increases as the taxable proportion of capital gains increases.

Solving the two marginal productivity conditions gives the firm's factor demand equations, of the general form

$$K^*(t) = K\left\{p(t), c(t), w(t)\right\}$$

$$L^*(t) = L\left\{p(t), c(t), w(t)\right\} \, ,$$

and the demand for investment goods is then given by

$$I^*(t) = \dot{K}^*(t) + \delta K^*(t).$$

Although these conditions hold at all points in time, the present model is not very dynamic, since only current variables enter the factor demand functions. The firm has solved an essentially static optimisation problem, and the only link between time periods is the capital stock series. The future course of profits or prices has no effect on current decisions, and past actions of the firm provide no constraint, since it is assumed that the capital stock can be adjusted instantaneously. This clearly unrealistic assumption has to be modified before a model suitable for empirical implementation is obtained, and a particular adjustment mechanism is discussed in the next section. Nevertheless the model is noteworthy for basing the demand for investment goods on profit maximising considerations. It also provides a description of the relationship between the demand for capital goods and the given technology via the production function, and a derivation of the relevant price of capital services, depending on the interest rate, the price of capital goods, and so forth. Again for empirical implementation an explicit form of the factor demand equation is required, which in turn requires an assumption about the functional form of the production function, and this too is discussed below.

## THE JORGENSON INVESTMENT FUNCTION

A Cobb-Douglas production function is assumed with $\alpha + \beta < 1$, making the firm's size determinate in a purely competitive world. So the marginal productivity conditions become

$$F_K = \alpha\frac{Q}{K} = \frac{c}{p}, \qquad F_L = \beta\frac{Q}{L} = \frac{w}{p},$$

and these, together with the production function, determine the output and factor input levels, then the demand for investment goods is given by $I = \dot{K} + \delta K$.

However investment projects take time to complete, so instantaneous achievement of the optimal capital stock position is not possible, and new machines ordered today will only be delivered at some future point in time. Accordingly, Jorgenson postulates an iterative decision process, whereby first $Q$ and $L$ are determined by the production function and the marginal productivity condition for labour, *given* the existing capital stock, then the desired capital stock $K^*$ is determined by the marginal productivity condition for capital. Thus at time $t$ the desired stock is given by

$$K_t^* = \alpha\frac{p_t Q_t}{c_t},$$

which is generally different from the existing stock, and the firm places orders sufficient to achieve $K_t^*$ by the time they are delivered. The firm attempts to adjust instantaneously, but is thwarted by unanticipated delivery lags.

Let new investment projects initiated or orders placed in period $t$ for expansion of capacity (not replacement) be $IN_t$. In the last period

$(t-1)$ the firm ordered sufficient to achieve $K^*_{t-1}$ by the time all new orders are delivered. So given that the procedure is well-established, in this period the firm only has to order enough new machines to make up the difference between the current and previous desired levels:

$$IN_t = K^*_t - K^*_{t-1} = \Delta K^*_t.$$

As investment projects take time to complete, let $\mu_j$ be the proportion which takes $j$ periods to complete. Then of orders placed this period, a proportion $\mu_0$ will be delivered immediately, a proportion $\mu_1$ will be delivered in the next period, $\mu_2$ in the period after that, and so on. If all orders are delivered (no bankruptcies among suppliers or cancellations) then $\Sigma \mu_j = 1$. The consequence is that current investment expenditure, $IE_t$, for expansion of capacity is a function of past orders and has the same coefficients, for a proportion $\mu_0$ of current orders are delivered this period, a proportion $\mu_1$ of the orders placed last period will also be delivered in the current period, a proportion $\mu_2$ of the orders placed two periods ago will be delivered this period too, and so on. Thus

$$IE_t = \sum_{j=0}^{\infty} \mu_j IN_{t-j} = \sum_{j=0}^{\infty} \mu_j \Delta K^*_{t-j},$$

and actual investment expenditure is a distributed lag function of current and past orders, or changes in desired capital stock. These delivery delays are assumed constant, so that if orders are (say) quadrupled, a proportion $\mu_0$ is still delivered immediately, $\mu_1$ in the next period, etc. If $\Delta K^*_t$ is negative the firm may start selling capital equipment, but its behaviour then is not described by this same distributed lag, so there is an assumption that $\Delta K^*_t > 0$.

Gross investment $I_t$ comprises $IE_t$ together with replacement investment, assumed to be proportional to the beginning capital stock $K_{t-1}$. Accordingly we now have

$$I_t = \sum_{j=0}^{\infty} \mu_j \Delta K^*_{t-j} + \delta K_{t-1}.$$

Finally, incorporating the determinants of desired capital stock, we obtain an equation for net investment, as follows:

$$I_t - \delta K_{t-1} = \sum_{j=0}^{\infty} \mu_j \Delta \left( \alpha \frac{pQ}{c} \right)_{t-j} = \mu(L) \Delta \left( \alpha \frac{pQ}{c} \right)_t .$$

At this point, the rational lag function is employed. Substituting $\mu(L) = \gamma(L)/\omega(L)$ and multiplying through by $\omega(L)$ gives

$$\omega(L)\{I_t - \delta K_{t-1}\} = \gamma(L) \Delta \left( \alpha \frac{pQ}{c} \right)_t .$$

Generally Jorgenson takes $\omega(L)$ to be a second-degree polynomial normalised by setting $\omega_0 = 1$, so the regression equation is

$$I_t - \delta K_{t-1} = \alpha \gamma(L) \Delta \left( \frac{pQ}{c} \right)_t - \omega_1 (I_{t-1} - \delta K_{t-2})$$

$$- \omega_2 (I_{t-2} - \delta K_{t-3}),$$

and a constant term is also added. In the first work (Jorgenson, 1963) $\gamma(L)$ has only one non-zero coefficient $\gamma_2$, but later (Jorgenson, 1965) there are up to three non-zero coefficients, $\gamma(L)$ for total durables manufacturing, for example, being of the form $\gamma_3 L^3 + \gamma_4 L^4 + \gamma_5 L^5$. In this latter case a change in one of the determinants of $K^*$ at a given point of time does not start to affect investment expenditures until three quarters later — generally quarterly data are employed. There are few formal criteria available to guide the choice of particular lag polynomials, and Jorgenson relies on the estimated standard error of the regression together with certain general restrictions derived from exploratory empirical research — in later work the degree of $\gamma(L)$ is limited to seven, with at most four non-zero coefficients, these being adjacent to one another, with the first coefficient positive.

As usual the derived equation will not fit the observations exactly so a disturbance term is added. Unfortunately Jorgenson provides no rationalisation for the disturbances (e.g. failures of profit maximisation, random variation in delivery times) but simply adds a general catch-all term to the estimating equation — no explanation is provided in terms of errors in the component structural equations of the model. Notice that if we add a disturbance $u_t$ to the original investment equation $I_t - \delta K_{t-1} = \mu(L)\Delta K_t^*$ then in multiplying through by the denominator $\omega(L)$ of the rational lag function we obtain

$$\omega(L)(I_t - \delta K_{t-1}) = \gamma(L)\Delta K_t^* + \omega(L)u_t$$

and it is this error term in the final equation which is assumed independent, i.e. $\omega(L)u_t = \epsilon_t$. If this assumption (that the original $u_t$ has the autoregressive structure $u_t + \omega_1 u_{t-1} + \omega_2 u_{t-2} = \epsilon_t$ with the same $\omega$-coefficients) is correct, then estimation can proceed by ordinary least squares. But if the original error term is independent, then multiplication by $\omega(L)$ will induce autocorrelation in the final error term, and ordinary least squares estimates will be inconsistent. The Durbin-Watson test was not designed for equations containing lagged values of the dependent variable, and when the lagged dependent variable is present the Durbin-Watson statistic is biased towards 2, so an alternative such as Durbin's $h$-test should be employed.

The capital stock series has to be constructed using data on $I_t$, an assumed value of $\delta$, and the relation

$$K_t = I_t + (1-\delta)K_{t-1} \, ,$$

for while benchmark observations on capital stock are available from Censuses of Production, quarterly data are not available. An estimate of $\delta$ is obtained by using this recursion relation and the investment series to interpolate between two capital stock benchmark figures — in the first work this gave a value of 0.025. There are then the alternative possibilities of leaving $\delta K_{t-1}$ as part of the dependent variable or of taking it to the right-hand side; in the latter case a regression estimate of $\delta$ is obtained together with the other coefficients. Jorgenson calls the former situation, where $-\delta K_{t-1}$ remains as part of the dependent variable with the value of $\delta$ obtained as above, the restricted case. The unrestricted case provides an estimate which is not constrained to equal 0.025, by estimating $\delta$ as the coefficient of $K_{t-1}$. The value obtained in this way can be used as a rough check on the value of $\delta$ used in calculating the capital stock series. However, the test is not a particularly strong one, since the assumed value of the depreciation parameter is built into the capital stock series, and one would not expect the estimated value to be far from it, no matter how inappropriate it was.

Finally, the exponent $\alpha$ in the Cobb-Douglas production function is estimated from the requirement that $\Sigma\mu_i = 1$. We have estimates of $\omega$'s and $(\alpha\gamma)$'s, and the sum of the $\mu$-coefficients is set equal to one by requiring that $\hat{\gamma}(1)/\hat{\omega}(1) = 1$, hence

$$\hat{\alpha} = \frac{\widehat{\alpha\gamma}(1)}{\hat{\omega}(1)} = \frac{\text{sum of coefficients on } \Delta\dfrac{pQ}{c} \text{ terms}}{1 + \hat{\omega}_1 + \hat{\omega}_2}$$

A simple illustration is provided by Jorgenson (1963), using data on total manufacturing (restricted case):

$$(I_t - \delta K_{t-1}) = \text{constant} + 1.524\,(I_{t-1} - \delta K_{t-2})$$
$$(0.099)$$

$$- 0.631\,(I_{t-2} - \delta K_{t-3})$$
$$(0.101)$$

$$+ 0.00106\,\Delta\frac{p_{t-2}\,Q_{t-2}}{c_{t-2}}, \quad R^2 = 0.942.$$
$$(0.0005)$$

The estimated lag functions are

$$\hat{\omega}(L) = 1 - 1.524\,L + 0.631\,L^2, \quad \widehat{\alpha\gamma}(L) = 0.00106\,L^2$$

hence $\hat{\alpha} = 0.00106/0.107 = 0.01$, which seems remarkably small.

Since the initial paper the emphasis has been on disaggregating the data. Jorgenson (1965) breaks total manufacturing into durables and non-durables and later work has applied the same model to 15 sub-industries of total manufacturing. (Jorgenson and Stephenson (1967a, 1967b, 1969a) — the first paper contains the regression results

and the second concentrates upon the implied $\mu$'s; the third is
concerned with anticipations data.) Jorgenson and Stephenson defend
their small estimates of $\alpha$ by arguing that the estimated value would
correspond to the relative share of capital in value added (cf. p.48) only
where desired and actual capital were equal, and that downward bias
may result from measurement errors in observed values of changes in
desired capital. Other arguments against estimating production function
parameters from this investment theory are discussed below. The results
provide some support for the neoclassical view that capital prices affect
investment decisions, although the influence of different components
of $K^*$ is restricted by the tight specification used by Jorgenson: some
further tests are also discussed below. Nevertheless, the effects of
interest rates, taxation and so forth can be derived from the estimates,
together with the paths of dynamic response to changes, by using $\hat{\alpha}$ to
obtain $\hat{\gamma}(L)$ and then calculating $\hat{\mu}(L)$ as illustrated on p.95. An average
lag between a change in the demand for capital stock and the
corresponding net investment can be calculated as $\Sigma j \mu_j$, which is
estimated as 6½ quarters in this example.

## CALCULATION OF POLICY EFFECTS

We now consider the estimation of the effect on investment of
alternative policy instruments. Attention is first centred on the
dynamic pattern of the response of gross investment expenditures $I_t$ to
a change in $K_t^*$, irrespective of the source of that change. This requires a
final equation that relates $I_t$ directly to $K_t^*$ and so allows for
replacement effects by solving out the $\delta K_{t-1}$ term. The "behavioural"
equation is

$$I_t = \mu(L)\Delta K_t^* + \delta K_{t-1}$$

and we also have the identity

$$I_t = \Delta K_t + \delta K_{t-1} \, ,$$

thus $\Delta K_t = \mu(L)\Delta K_t^*$ and so $K_t = \mu(L)K_t^*$, neglecting the constant of integration. Hence

$$I_t = \mu(L)\Delta K_t^* + \delta\mu(L)K_{t-1}^*.$$

Now suppose that $K^*$ has been constant for some time, but it then changes to a new level, following a change in an interest rate or a tax parameter, for example. Suppose for convenience that the difference between the old and new levels of $K^*$ is equal to one unit. We seek the coefficients $\xi_\tau$ giving the effect on $I$ after $\tau$ periods. Since $K^*$ is constant except for the period in which the change occurs, $\Delta K^*$ is zero except for that period, when it has a value of one. Thus the contribution to $\xi_\tau$ of the first term on the right-hand side of the preceding equation is simply $\mu_\tau$. The contribution of the second term requires the calculation of partial sums of the $\mu$'s, and remembering that $K^*$ appears with a one-period lag, the contribution to $\xi_1$ is $\delta\mu_0$, to $\xi_2$ is $\delta(\mu_0+\mu_1)$, and so on. Thus in general

$$\xi_\tau = \mu_\tau + \delta \sum_{j=0}^{\tau-1} \mu_j,$$

taking the summation to be zero when $\tau=0$. Recalling that $\mu_j$ represents the proportion of orders which are delivered after $j$ periods, we expect that $\mu_j \to 0$ as $j \to \infty$; also all orders are delivered at some time, so

$$\sum_{j=0}^{\tau} \mu_j \to 1 \text{ as } \tau \to \infty.$$

It therefore follows that

$$\xi_\tau \to \delta \text{ as } \tau \to \infty,$$

that is, a change in $K^*$ has a long-run effect equal to the replacement proportion. If $K^*$ increases to a higher constant level, and subsequently investment occurs to adjust actual $K$ to $K^*$, then once this is achieved replacement investment is all that is occurring, and this is higher than before by a proportion $\delta$ of the increase in $K^*$ (and $K$).

To assess the effect on gross investment expenditures of an interest rate change we seek

$$\frac{\partial I}{\partial r} = \frac{\partial I}{\partial K^*} \frac{\partial K^*}{\partial r}$$

and $\xi_\tau \ \partial K^*/\partial r$ gives the effect $\tau$ periods later, the long-run effect being $\delta \ \partial K^*/\partial r$. Recall that $K^* = \alpha \, pQ/c$, with $c$ a function of $r$, hence $\partial K^*/\partial r$ is given by $(\partial K^*/\partial c)(\partial c/\partial r)$. Differentiating

$$\frac{\partial K^*}{\partial c} = -\alpha \frac{pQ}{c^2} \, , \, \frac{\partial c}{\partial r} = q \, \frac{1-uv_2}{1-u}$$

therefore

$$\frac{\partial K^*}{\partial r} = \alpha \frac{pQ}{c^2} \, q \, \frac{1-uv_2}{1-u} \, . \qquad \bullet$$

This can be calculated from an estimate of $\alpha$ and actual values of the variables $p$, $Q$, $c$, $q$, $u$ and $v_2$. Since these values vary, it is necessary to choose a time on which to base the calculation. Jorgenson (1965, Table 2.8) calculates the effect of changes in market conditions ($r$, $q$, $p$) and tax parameters ($u$, $v_1$, $v_2$) using the values of the variables that held at the end of the sample period (fourth quarter, 1962). Jorgenson (1963, Table 3) presents long run responses ($\delta \ \partial K^*/\partial r$, etc.) using both average and end-period values of the variables.

Likewise, *elasticities* can be obtained. However, this turns out to be uninteresting. For example, we have

$$\frac{\partial K^*}{\partial q} = \frac{\partial K^*}{\partial c} \frac{\partial c}{\partial q} = -\alpha \frac{pQ}{c^2} \, (\delta + r),$$

so the elasticity with respect to $q$ is

$$\frac{\partial \log K^*}{\partial \log q} = -\alpha \frac{pQ}{c^2} \, (\delta + r) \, \frac{q}{K^*} = -1.$$

The elasticity of capital stock with respect to the relative price ratio is also one, as is the elasticity with respect to output, which is easily seen by noting that in $K^* = \alpha(p/c)Q$, the exponents of $p/c$ and $Q$ are 1. These follow from the unit elasticity of substitution in the Cobb-Douglas production function, which is part of Jorgenson's maintained hypothesis – an assumption underlying his basic tests which is maintained and not itself tested. Jorgenson's work estimates the time shape of responses but these unitary elasticities are built into his model. Critics have suggested that this should be an open question, and to this we now turn.

### TESTS OF JORGENSON'S MAINTAINED HYPOTHESES

As already observed, a noteworthy feature of Jorgenson's model is the explicit relation between investment demand and the underlying technology via the production function. Although a Cobb-Douglas production function is then assumed, other more general possibilities exist, and if the assumption that $\sigma = 1$ is relaxed then it is no longer the case that the elasticities with respect to relative prices and output are both equal to 1. Adopting a CES production function as an alternative,

$$Q = \gamma \left\{ \delta K^{-\rho} + (1-\delta)L^{-\rho} \right\}^{-\nu/\rho}$$

the marginal productivity condition for capital is (cf. p.69)

$$K^{1+\rho} = \nu \delta \gamma^{-\rho/\nu} Q^{1+\rho/\nu} \frac{p}{c}.$$

Since $\sigma = 1/(1+\rho)$, this gives as the equation for desired capital stock

$$K^* = A \left( \frac{p}{c} \right)^{\sigma} Q^{\sigma(1+\rho/\nu)} = A \left( \frac{p}{c} \right)^{E_p} Q^{E_Q} \text{ say,}$$

where $E_p$ is the elasticity of $K^*$ with respect to $p/c$, equal to $\sigma$, and $E_Q$ is the elasticity with respect to output, equal to $\sigma + (1-\sigma)/\nu$.

Only in the Cobb-Douglas case where $\sigma = 1$ is it necessarily true that

$E_p = E_Q = 1$, although it is true that $E_Q = 1$ for any $\sigma$ if there are constant returns to scale ($\nu = 1$). The combination $E_p = 0$ and $E_Q = 1$ takes us back to the simple accelerator.

Eisner and Nadiri (1968) point out that $E_p$ and $E_Q$ can be estimated in this more general specification, thus providing a test of Jorgenson's maintained hypothesis that both are equal to 1. Then one matter of interest is the effect of these alternative assumptions and estimates on the policy conclusions. The relation between net investment and changes in the determinants of $K^*$ is estimated by Eisner and Nadiri in first-differenced logarithmic form:

$$\Delta \log K_t = \mu(L)\Delta \log K_t^*.$$

This form is convenient since the coefficients then give estimated elasticities directly, although the differences between the linear and log forms are small (Eisner and Nadiri, 1970). Taking the log of the above expression for $K^*$, the terms in relative prices and output enter separately, and using the rational lag function modified to permit these two determinants of $K^*$ to have possibly different lag response functions, we have

$$\omega(L)\Delta \log K_t = \gamma_p(L)\Delta \log \frac{p}{c} + \gamma_Q(L)\Delta \log Q.$$

With the same specifications for $\omega$ and $\gamma$ as used by Jorgenson and Stephenson, the estimating equation is

$$\Delta \log K_t = \sum_{i=n}^{k} \left\{ \gamma_{pi}\Delta \log \left(\frac{p}{c}\right)_{t-i} + \gamma_{Qi}\Delta \log Q_{t-i} \right\}$$

$$- \omega_1 \Delta \log K_{t-1} - \omega_2 \Delta \log K_{t-2}.$$

(Eisner and Nadiri also question the Jorgenson-Stephenson restrictions on $\gamma(L)$, in which $n$ is taken to be 3 or 4.)

There are two major consequences of this formulation. First, the long-run elasticities are estimated as

$$E_p = \frac{\Sigma\hat{\gamma}_{pi}}{1+\hat{\omega}_1+\hat{\omega}_2}, E_Q = \frac{\Sigma\hat{\gamma}_{Qi}}{1+\hat{\omega}_1+\hat{\omega}_2},$$

and not only are they not constrained to 1, they are also permitted to differ from each other. In this framework, Eisner and Nadiri first test whether the elasticities are the same, and then whether this common value is in fact 1. The simplest test of Jorgenson's maintained hypothesis that the elasticity with respect to $pQ/c$ is 1 is provided by setting $\gamma_{pi} = \gamma_{Qi}$ and estimating

$$\Delta\log K_t = \sum_{i=n}^{k} \gamma_i \log \left(\frac{pQ}{c}\right)_{t-i} - \omega_1 \Delta\log K_{t-1} - \omega_2 \Delta\log K_{t-2},$$

then testing whether

$$\frac{\Sigma\hat{\gamma}_i}{1+\hat{\omega}_1+\hat{\omega}_2} = 1.$$

The second consequence is that having entered $p/c$ and $Q$ with separate lag polynomials, we permit the time responses of net investment to changes in relative prices and output to differ, although Jorgenson's policy analyses assume that they are the same. It is an empirical question whether net investment reacts with a different delay to an output change than to a change in a tax rate, since the dynamic specification is not itself supported by an economic model. Thus it should not be subjected to needless restrictions in estimation.

Bischoff (1969) relaxes a further maintained hypothesis which relates to the specification of the error terms, namely that the errors in the final estimating equation are free of autocorrelation. (Eisner and Nadiri (1968), for comparability with Jorgenson, also assume independent errors.) Observe that adding an error term $u_t$ to the exact equation $\Delta K_t = \mu(L)\Delta K_t^*$ produces a moving average error of the form $u_t + \omega_1 u_{t-1} + \omega_2 u_{t-2}$ in the final estimating equation, as noted above (p.104). Similarly, if a multiplicative error $\exp(u_t)$ is added to the equation for $K^*$ to represent the influence of omitted variables on the determination of desired capital stock, then the regression equation for $\Delta\log K_t$ has a disturbance term $\gamma(L)\,\Delta u_t$. These and other possibilities result in a suspicion of autocorrelated errors which, if correct, renders OLS estimates inconsistent. As a first approximation, Bischoff allows the error term $w_t$ in the levels equation (rather than the first difference version)

$$\log K_t = \ldots - \omega_1 \log K_{t-1} - \omega_2 \log K_{t-2} + w_t$$

to be a first-order autoregression:

$$w_t = \rho w_{t-1} + \epsilon_t.$$

Only if $\rho = 0$ are OLS estimates of the levels equation consistent; only if $\rho = 1$ does OLS estimation using first differences provide consistent estimates. Note that this assumption is only one stage better than the previous maintained hypothesis as it uses only a first-order autoregression. However, if the error is truly of this form, then joint estimation of the regression coefficients and $\rho$ provides consistent and efficient estimates together with accurate standard errors.

A further difficulty is the problem of accurately estimating and testing the ratio estimates of elasticities given above. In general, when estimating an equation whose coefficients are functions of the structural parameters, it is necessary to unscramble the regression coefficients to obtain structural parameter estimates. When this involves taking ratios of functions of regression coefficients where the denominator is quite small (in some cases $1 + \hat{\omega}_1 + \hat{\omega}_2$ is close to zero), the calculation is rather unreliable, since a small discrepancy due to sampling errors in a relatively small denominator will have a substantial effect on the ratio. Thus we expect not to be able to estimate ratios of this kind very accurately. The empirical results yield estimated elasticities which have high standard errors, and this can largely be attributed to the expression in the denominator being small and itself subject to error.

After much argument[1] which need not be repeated here, the estimated price elasticity appears to be significantly below 1 (of the order of 0.1-0.2), contrary to Jorgenson's maintained hypothesis, and the overall role of relative prices is rather slight. The estimated elasticity with respect to output also tends to be below 1, though the departures from 1 are not so significant. Lastly the lag distributions with respect to price and output effects do appear to differ, with the response to relative price changes being rather slower than the response to output changes. However, all these estimates are derived from equations in which output is treated as exogenous, and we finally consider the effect of this specification error.

## ENDOGENEITY AND DYNAMICS

As we have seen, the approach adopted by Jorgenson and his forerunners separates the calculation of the firm's desired capital stock $K^*$ from the determination of investment expenditures over time. In Jorgenson's case, the value of $K^*$ results from a profit maximisation calculation, and this is then translated into an investment path by unforeseen delivery lags. The assumption that delivery delays continue to surprise the firm seems rather unlikely, for having regularly observed that orders for new machinery are not fulfilled instantaneously, a sensible manager will begin to take this fact into account. More generally, as Gould (1969) points out, the firm will recognise the interactions between the calculation of $K^*$ and the adjustment process, possibly regarding the latter as a constraint in profit maximisation. Thus the optimal behaviour in the static model will not be optimal in a dynamic world.

To illustrate this interaction in the context of Jorgenson's model, assume that the exogenous variables (interest rate, prices and so forth) have remained constant for some time, so that the firm has adjusted to its equilibrium capital stock position. Output and input levels are $Q_0$,

---

[1] Eisner and Nadiri (1968, 1970), Bischoff (1969), Jorgenson and Stephenson (1969b); see also Jorgenson (1971) and Klein (1974).

$K_0$, and $L_0$, say, as given by the solution of the marginal productivity conditions and the production function, and investment expenditure is incurred only for the replacement of worn-out machines, at a constant rate. Now suppose that the interest rate falls to a new value $r_1$, which the firm expects to hold for some time. The long-run equilibrium or comparative static solution is given by the values $Q_1$, $K_1$, and $L_1$, obtained in terms of the exogenous variable values by solving the three equations as before. Since there are no adjustment costs, the optimal strategy for the firm is to get to this new position as quickly as possible, and orders should be immediately placed to increase capital stock from $K_0$ to $K_1$. Investment expenditure for expansion of capacity, *IE*, then takes the values $\mu_j(K_1 - K_0)$, $j = 0,1,\ldots$, over the next few periods. During this interregnum, the capital stock is constrained by the rate at which new machines can be delivered, and the firm chooses the optimal values of $Q$ and $L$, given $K$. However, in the Jorgenson model, the firm first solves the labour marginal productivity condition and the production function for $Q$ and $L$, given the existing capital stock, and then uses this value of $Q$ to calculate $K^*$. At the new interest rate $r_1$, the values of $Q$ and $L$ calculated in terms of $K_0$ will be below the equilibrium values $Q_1$ and $L_1$, hence the resulting $K^*$ value will be below $K_1$, and a sub-optimal quantity of investment projects will be initiated. Thus the adjustment to the new equilibrium position is rather slower than is optimal. Indeed, if there are no deliveries of new machines until two periods have elapsed, as in Jorgenson's empirical work, then the second round of adjustment will not occur until then, for the capital stock remains at $K_0$, and $Q$ and $L$ remain at the values given by $K_0$ and $r_1$, hence $K^*$ does not change again, and no further orders are placed to move towards $K_1$ until the capital stock changes from $K_0$ when the first new delivery arrives.

The conclusion is that the investment path given by the Jorgenson approach is not consistent with profit-maximising behaviour. In this dynamic framework, output is an inappropriate determinant of desired capital stock and hence investment, for it is itself an endogenous variable. Note that this criticism is independent of the particular production function adopted, and applies equally to the work of Eisner and Nadiri. What is required is an expression for $K^*$ entirely in terms of exogenous variables, in order that a genuine reduced form equation can be derived, or a recognition of the joint dependence of the endogenous variables.

As a further point of interest, we can ask how such a reduced form equation would be interpreted in the Jorgenson context, in particular with respect to the coefficient $\alpha$. The reduced form expression for $K$ for a profit-maximising perfectly competitive Cobb-Douglas ($\alpha+\beta<1$) firm is given by the solution of the three-equation system on p.48, which in the notation of this chapter is as follows:

$$K = (A\alpha^{1-\beta} \beta^{\beta} pc^{-(1-\beta)} w^{-\beta})^{1/1-\alpha-\beta}.$$

In the present situation, this equation determines $K^*$, before delivery lags set in. The corresponding Jorgenson equation is $K^* = \alpha(pQ/c)$. In either case, an investment equation is obtained by imposing a lag function $\mu(L)$, although this is not our main concern. However it might overcome the problem of simultaneity, for if $Q$ only appears in the investment function with a lag of at least two periods, then it can be treated as a predetermined variable under appropriate assumptions about the error term. If firms were behaving optimally, but an investigator thought that they were obeying the Jorgenson $K^*$ relation, then the estimated equation would be mis-specified, erroneously including $Q$ and excluding $w$, and imposing unwarranted restrictions on the coefficients. It is difficult to say what are the effects of such specification errors, but even if they were zero, the interpretation of the constant term or scale factor is erroneous. The scale factor which the investigator would interpret as an estimate of $\alpha$ is really an estimate of $(A\alpha^{1-\beta} \beta^{\beta})^{1/1-\alpha-\beta}$. If $Q$ is measured in appropriate units so that $A=1$, then for $\alpha+\beta$ not too far below 1 this scale factor is a very small number (.004 if $\alpha = 0.3$, $\beta = 0.6$), and if $A$ is not equal to 1, or specification errors have an influence, then the scale factor will be a mixture of these various effects, and almost certainly not equal to $\alpha$. Thus the reason why one would not wish to estimate the parameters of production functions from Jorgenson's theory of investment behaviour is that they would be subject to specification error.

These criticisms are concerned with the properties of Jorgenson's sequential decision procedure, while other assumptions about the absence of adjustment costs and the exclusive role of delivery delays as the source of dynamics have been accepted. These are clearly oversimplifying assumptions, and more realistic models need to incorporate costs of adjustment, the irreversibility of investment and uncertainty: for a theoretical treatment and survey of the evidence see Nickell (1978). Investment studies typically treat labour as a completely variable factor, despite the evidence from employment studies, while employment studies typically take capital stock as given. A neoclassical model of simultaneous decisions about factor input levels has already been presented, and in the next section we discuss an approach to the joint determination of capital and labour inputs in the face of a particular cost of adjustment function utilised in empirical work by Nadiri and Rosen (1969, 1973) and Brechling (1975).

## DYNAMIC FACTOR DEMANDS

We first present a simple adjustment cost model that leads, as we shall see, to the flexible accelerator. It is assumed that the firm chooses the level of capital input $K_t$ in order to minimise the weighted sum of "disequilibrium" and "adjustment" costs:

$$C_t = a_1(K_t - K_t^*)^2 + a_2(K_t - K_{t-1})^2.$$

The first term on the right-hand side represents the costs incurred by being away from the optimum position $K_t^*$. Of course $K_t^*$ is the result of a profit-maximising or cost-minimising calculation in the absence of adjustment costs, and that calculation will generally yield an explicit expression for the disequilibrium costs. However the assumptions that these costs are a quadratic function of the gap $K_t - K_t^*$, and that the firm employs a two-stage decision process of first calculating $K_t^*$ and then $K_t$, are adopted in order to focus on the new element in the problem. This is the second term on the right-hand side, representing the cost of adjusting capital input from the preceding level $K_{t-1}$ to the new level $K_t$. The cost is assumed to be positive whatever the direction of change from the previous value, and the quadratic formulation implies that there is an increasing marginal cost of adjustment. To find the value of $K_t$ that minimises $C_t$ we equate the first partial derivative to zero:

$$2a_1(K_t - K_t^*) + 2a_2(K_t - K_{t-1}) = 0.$$

On rearranging, this gives

$$K_t = \frac{a_1}{a_1 + a_2} K_t^* + \frac{a_2}{a_1 + a_2} K_{t-1},$$

and on setting $\gamma = a_2/(a_1 + a_2)$ we obtain

$$K_t - K_{t-1} = (1-\gamma)(K_t^* - K_{t-1}),$$

the flexible accelerator or partial adjustment hypothesis. This is thus seen to result from the quadratic cost minimisation hypothesis, as was first pointed out in this context by Eisner and Strotz (1963). If adjustment costs are relatively important the coefficient $a_2$ will be relatively large, which implies a value of $\gamma$ near to 1 and relatively slow adjustment. Clearly if $a_2 = 0$ there are no costs of adjustment and the firm moves immediately to the desired position $K_t^*$.

To include the possibility that there is *no* input that can be adjusted costlessly, this model has been generalised to the case of several inputs. The main points can be made in the two-variable case, so we write

$$\begin{bmatrix} K_t - K_{t-1} \\ L_t - L_{t-1} \end{bmatrix} = \begin{bmatrix} \theta_{11} & \theta_{12} \\ \theta_{21} & \theta_{22} \end{bmatrix} \begin{bmatrix} K_t^* - K_{t-1} \\ L_t^* - L_{t-1} \end{bmatrix}.$$

Both factors of production are now subject to adjustment costs, and the off-diagonal elements in the coefficient matrix imply the existence of short-run substitution possibilities, and that an imbalance in one factor will generally cause adjustments to both factor input levels. Brechling (1975) imposes no further restrictions on the adjustment coefficients, while Nadiri and Rosen (1973) consider the consequences of the requirement that the firm remains on its production function, with output exogenous. In their case factor utilisation rates are entered as separate arguments in the production function, but their approach can be illustrated in the present 2×2 case, albeit rather unrealistically. Assume a Cobb-Douglas production function, and for the moment take $Q$, $K$ and $L$ to represent the logarithms of output and inputs (the adjustment hypothesis then being interpreted in ratio form). Since the output level is given, and the firm must remain on its production function, we have

$$\alpha K_t + \beta L_t = \alpha K_t^* + \beta L_t^*.$$

Immediately there must be compensatory adjustments, as

$$\alpha(K_t - K_t^*) + \beta(L_t - L_t^*) = 0.$$

The partial adjustment mechanism can be written

$$\begin{bmatrix} K_t - K_t^* \\ L_t - L_t^* \end{bmatrix} = \begin{bmatrix} \theta_{11} - 1 & \theta_{12} \\ \theta_{21} & \theta_{22} - 1 \end{bmatrix} \begin{bmatrix} K_t^* - K_{t-1} \\ L_t^* - L_{t-1} \end{bmatrix},$$

and for the immediately preceding equation to hold in general we require that

$$\alpha(\theta_{11} - 1) + \beta\theta_{21} = 0$$

$$\alpha\theta_{12} + \beta(\theta_{22} - 1) = 0$$

This implies the restriction $\theta_{21}/(1-\theta_{11}) = (1-\theta_{22})/\theta_{12}$, and that this last coefficient matrix is singular. The situation is illustrated in Figure 13, where point $A$ represents the desired position at time $t$ and point $B$ the actual position. In this case $\theta_{11} < \theta_{22}$, and capital input cannot be adjusted rapidly hence labour input is "overadjusted".

Finally, we can consider what the existence of interrelated factor demand functions implies for the behaviour of a single factor input over

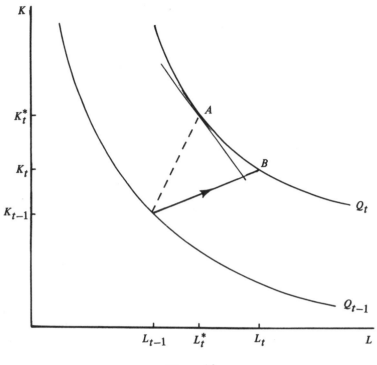

*Figure 13*

time, as described by its final equation. The simultaneous partial adjustment model can be written

$$K_t = \theta_{11}K_t^* + \theta_{12}L_t^* + (1-\theta_{11})K_{t-1} - \theta_{12}L_{t-1}$$

$$L_t = \theta_{21}K_t^* + \theta_{22}L_t^* - \theta_{21}K_{t-1} + (1-\theta_{22})L_{t-1} \, .$$

To obtain the final equation for $K_t$, containing the starred variables and lagged values of $K$ but not $L$, we lag the first equation, multiply through by $(1-\theta_{22})$, and subtract the result from the first equation. The resulting expression for $K_t - (1-\theta_{22})K_{t-1}$ contains the terms $-\theta_{12}L_{t-1} + (1-\theta_{22})\theta_{12}L_{t-2}$ on the right-hand side, which can be eliminated by using the second equation, lagged one period, to give an expression for $\theta_{12}L_{t-1}$; this introduces among other things a further term in $K_{t-2}$. In this way we obtain the expression

$$K_t = f(K_t^*, L_t^*, K_{t-1}^*, L_{t-1}^*) - \omega_1 K_{t-1} - \omega_2 K_{t-2},$$

$$\omega_1 = \theta_{11} + \theta_{22} - 2, \quad \omega_2 = (1-\theta_{11})(1-\theta_{22}) - \theta_{12}\theta_{21},$$

hence the one-period lag in the joint adjustment model implies a two-period lag in the equation for $K$ alone (except when the Nadiri-Rosen production function restrictions are imposed, for these give $\omega_2 = 0$). The first term on the right-hand side involves the determinants of the starred variables (prices and other exogenous variables), current and lagged, and so we have a further interpretation of the Jorgenson-type investment function with $\omega(L)$ of second degree, namely as a form of solution of this interrelated factor demand model. Nevertheless the justification for the presence of these lags is quite different.

In this last section we have begun to consider dynamic simultaneous equation models, although in the simplest possible form, having but two equations and a one-period lag. Such systems are considered more generally in the final chapter, and to obtain generality without a mass of algebra a further mathematical technique is introduced. However we have already seen an example of one of the general results, namely that a simultaneous equation system with low-order dynamics implies a higher-order distributed lag model for the endogenous variables taken one at a time.

# IV

# SIMULTANEOUS EQUATION SYSTEMS

## INTRODUCTION

In the preceding chapters, we have considered from time to time the problems that arise when it is explicitly acknowledged that the particular behavioural relationship under consideration is embedded in a system of equations describing the simultaneous interactions of the relevant variables. Thus we considered the consequences for estimates of the consumption function from aggregate time series data of the fact that income is not an exogenous variable but is jointly determined with consumption in a more extensive system of equations. Likewise, the theory of the firm was brought to bear on the production and investment decisions by postulating a perfectly competitive firm simultaneously deciding its output and input levels, and subsequently its demand for capital goods, in the face of given prices, wages, and interest rates. Nevertheless attention remained concentrated on the particular behavioural relationship itself, and the model constructed around it was often relatively simple. Other components of income were not considered at the same time as consumption, nor was the determination of prices, wages, and interest rates considered along with production and investment.

In this chapter we discuss complete simultaneous equation systems. In applied work generally, as in econometric theory and methods texts whenever illustrative examples are constructed, examples fall into two main groups, and so it is here. First there are complete models of the markets for individual commodities or groups of commodities — demand and supply models — and we consider a single example of an agricultural commodity. Then we consider the construction and use of national income determination systems — macroeconometric models.

Our emphasis is on the general application of such models, rather than the details of the structure of any particular model, for the specifications of operational models are continually changing, and in any case a full account of one of the large national income forecasting models currently in use would itself be of book-length.

## A DEMAND AND SUPPLY MODEL: THE U.S. WATERMELON MARKET

The study of the watermelon market by Suits (1955) was one of the first in which both demand and supply schedules were estimated for the same market, and it also provides an interesting twist to the cobweb model. Subsequently the model was reformulated as a causal chain by Wold (1958), and subjected to forecasting tests by l'Esperance (1964).

The first equation is a crop supply schedule, which essentially describes planting decisions, and relates the total number of watermelons available for harvest $Q$, to various prices in the previous season. These are the "own" price of watermelons $P$, and the prices of two commodities competing for farm space: cotton $(C)$ and other vegetables $(T)$. The estimated equation is

$$Q = 769 + 0.587 \, P_{-1} - 0.320 \, C_{-1} - 0.141 \, T_{-1} \qquad (1)$$
$$\phantom{Q = 769 + 0}(.156) \qquad (.095) \qquad (.238)$$

(the subscript $-1$ indicates a one-period lagged value). All equations are fitted using logarithms of the variables, so that the coefficients are estimated elasticities, thus the price elasticity of crop supply is about 0.6. For convenience the coefficients of dummy variables relating to World War II and government cotton policy are not reported here.

While the crop supply given by this equation is the quantity of watermelons available for harvest, the actual harvesting decision is influenced by current prices — if there is an insufficient margin, the crop is left unharvested. The number of watermelons harvested $X$, cannot of course exceed the crop $Q$, but is otherwise determined by the current price measured relative to the farm wage rate $W$, thus

$$X = -118 + 0.237 \, P/W + 1.205 \, Q \quad \text{or} \qquad (2a)$$
$$\phantom{X = -118 + 0}(.110) \qquad (.114)$$

$$X = Q \qquad (2b)$$

whichever is smaller. The first alternative is estimated by ignoring all years in which no unharvested crop is reported. The price elasticity of harvested supply is considerably smaller than that of crop supply, as might be expected, and the proportion of the crop harvested increases as the crop increases; note however that the coefficient of $Q$ is not significantly different from 1. This formulation is an early example of what subsequently became known as limited dependent variable models. That is, the value of $X$ determined by equation (2a) is only observed if $X < Q$, or, adding a disturbance term $u$ to (2a) and substituting from the right-hand side, $X$ is only observed if $u$ is less than the quantity estimated as $118 - 0.237\, P/W - 0.205\, Q$. The technical difficulty that arises is that the properties of estimates based on those observations for which $u$ *is* less than this quantity cannot rest on the assumption $E(u) = 0$, but further consideration is beyond our present scope.

The demand equation relates the current (farm) price to *per capita* disposable income $Y/N$, and *per capita* market supply $X/N$, together with an index of freight costs $F$:

$$P = -140 + 1.530\, Y/N - 1.110\, X/N - 0.682\, F. \qquad (3)$$
$$(.088) \qquad (.246) \qquad (.183)$$

Rewriting this equation with demand, $X/N$, on the left-hand side yields a derived estimate of the price elasticity of demand of $-1/1.110 = -0.9$, and an estimated income elasticity of $1.530/1.110 = 1.4$.

The endogenous variables are $Q$, $X$, and $P$; the justification for treating $Y$ and $W$ as exogenous is that the watermelon market not only represents a very small share of national income but also has a relative small influence, via the demand for labour, on farm wages. The first equation was estimated by OLS, as all the explanatory variables are predetermined, using data for the years 1919-1951. The remaining two equations contain endogenous variables on the right-hand side, and so were estimated by limited information maximum likelihood, a method applicable to overidentified simultaneous equations taken one at a time (and asymptotically equivalent to 2SLS). Observations on $X$ were not available in the early part of the sample period, so these equations were estimated for 1930-1951.

The dynamic structure of the model is different from that of the simple cobweb model, in which price and quantity are sequentially determined. Instead, the previous value of $P$ determines the current value of production $Q$, which in turn gives a kinked harvest supply schedule, and this in conjunction with the demand schedule gives the quantity sold $X$ and the new price. Nevertheless, a final equation for $P$ can be obtained as usual. On eliminating $X$ and $Q$ from equations (1), (2a), and (3) we obtain a final equation relating current price to its lagged value and a function of other exogenous variables, $H$ say, as follows:

$$P_t = -0.622 P_{t-1} + H_t.$$

If the values of the variables are such that (2b) is relevant, then the final equation becomes

$$P_t = -0.652 P_{t-1} + H_t^*.$$

Whether one equation or the other or some mixture of the two provides a description of the behaviour of prices over time, the system clearly is stable, approaching equilibrium in an oscillatory fashion. It is difficult to think of a situation in which a proportion of the crop is persistently left unharvested as an equilibrium position, although it could easily arise in the present formulation as a result of high wage rates. One might imagine that in a genuine equilibrium situation farmers would take such factors into account and ensure that the complete crop was harvested, which suggests that in the general situation the lagged wage rate might appear as a further explanatory variable in equation (1), as a proxy for expected wages in the same way that lagged prices are proxies for expected prices.

The simple cobweb model provides an elementary example of recursive systems, in which there is a unique causal ordering of endogenous variables rather than a joint determination involving simultaneous interactions. In the simplest version the quantity supplied depends on the previous period's price, and this quantity determines the current price via the demand schedule. The causal sequence is from last period's price to this period's quantity, to this period's price to next period's quantity, and so on, and for this to be a truly unidirectional sequence, with no feedback, it is also required that the disturbances in the demand and supply functions be independent of one another. This is likely to be a reasonable approximation in the context of an agricultural commodity model, since the random influences on supply are likely to be quite distinct from random influences on consumer behaviour, and to be separated from them in time. Under these assumptions OLS provides consistent estimates.

Wold (1958) reformulates the present model as a recursive system. The supply relation remains as Suits' equation (1), already a single causal relation. The remaining equations are reformulated to provide descriptions of the behaviour of the separate economic agents: merchants who regulate the price, and consumers who determine the level of demand. Suppliers, merchants and consumers are held to be autonomous, in the usual sense "that changes in the behaviour of one group do not necessarily bring about a change in the behaviour pattern of the other groups". Then, in the absence of feedback and with uncorrelated disturbance terms, the equations can be estimated by OLS.

Consumer demand is denoted by $X^*$, given by the harvest $X$ when only part of the crop is harvested, but unknown in the six years when $X = Q$. Again, a limited dependent variable formulation might now be more appropriate. A general cost of living index, $PI$, is introduced, so that *per capita* demand is determined by the relative price of watermelons and real *per capita* income:[1]

$$\frac{X^*}{N} = -1.087 - \underset{(.148)}{0.205} \frac{P}{PI} + \underset{(.209)}{0.429} \frac{Y}{N.PI} \qquad (2')$$

[1] Standard errors are not reported by Wold, and all the values given here result from my computations, using his data. There are small differences in the third decimal place of our coefficient values. Suits and Wold also differ in the coding of the logarithmic variables, but this only affects the size and not the sign of the constant term.

The price mechanism is influenced by the difference between demand and supply, and real *per capita* income:

$$\frac{P}{PI} = -1.285 + 0.266 \left[ \left( \frac{X^*}{N} \right)_{-1} - \frac{Q}{N} \right] + 1.216 \frac{Y}{N.PI} \qquad (3')$$
$$\phantom{\frac{P}{PI} = -1.285 + } (.420) \phantom{\left[ \left( \frac{X^*}{N} \right)_{-1} - \frac{Q}{N} \right] + } (.163)$$

The one-year lag on $X^*/N$ results from the argument that in fixing the current price, merchants have in mind expected or anticipated demand and supply, and whereas $Q$ will be known as planting has already taken place, demand is expected to continue at the level of the preceding year: this seems to provide another example of *ad hoc* dynamics. Again however we have a forerunner of recent developments in "disequilibrium econometrics", in which prices do not adjust sufficiently rapidly to equate demand and supply in every period, but nevertheless rise or fall in response to excess demand or supply. Real income is included on the grounds that with increasing income, "there is more room for margins between price and production cost", and as an indicator of merchants' salary expenses.

The causal ordering is $Q, P, X^*$. However it is seen that once attention is paid to standard errors, the general specification is not well supported by the data. Various forecasting exercises have been conducted with these models by l'Esperance (1964). First, forecasts obtained by solving Suits' structural equations were better than those obtained from a directly estimated reduced form: such comparisons are discussed in general terms below. Secondly, Suits' interdependent system provided more accurate forecasts than Wold's recursive version of the model, suggesting that the specification of the interdependent system is a better approximation in this case. Now that we have looked rather more closely at the lack of support for Wold's hypotheses offered by the data, this last finding is not surprising.

## MACROECONOMETRIC MODELS

We concentrate on the general principles of the construction and use of large-scale economy-wide models, and leave aside the detailed specifications of particular models, for there is little to be gained by singling out a current model and repeating at what would be considerable length the details of its equations, coefficients, and so forth. The one exception to this rule is a six-equation example discussed shortly, which also suggests that the cost of presenting the details of a much larger-scale model outweighs the benefits. The construction of many macroeconometric models is based on Keynesian theory and its developments, and the main uses are forecasting and policy analysis.

Nerlove (1966) describes, in summary form, the features of twenty-five statistical macro models, covering nine countries and ranging from the early models of Tinbergen (1939, 1951) and Klein (1950) to the massive Brookings-SSRC model of the U.S. economy (Duesenberry *et al.*, 1965, 1969; Fromm and Klein, 1975). Since this survey was undertaken models have expanded and proliferated beyond the compass of a single survey article. From time to time in both the U.K. and the U.S. conferences or symposia are organised at which the various national models are presented and discussed. For the U.S., see for example Hickman (1972), the symposium "Econometric model performance: comparative simulation studies of models of the U.S. economy" in the *International Economic Review*, 1974-75, and Fromm and Klein (1975); for the U.K. see Renton (1975), for medium term models Worswick and Blackaby (1974) and for comparative simulations and policy analyses Laury *et al.* (1978) and Posner (1978). In the U.K. the first series of published forecasts based on an operational macroeconometric model was begun by the London Business School in 1966, using a model developed by Professor Ball and his co-workers from the original quarterly U.K. model of Klein, Ball, Hazelwood and Vandome (1961); forecasts from the LBS model are presented quarterly in the *Sunday Times*. Also the forecasts published by the National Institute of Economic and Social Research in their quarterly *National Institute Economic Review* have gradually made more use of a fully specified model. The largest U.K. model is that of the Treasury, whose forecasts are published in *Economic Trends* and *Economic Progress Report*. Since the Bray amendment to the Industry Act of 1975 this model has been publicly available, and the forecasts of the ITEM (Independent Treasury Economic Model) Club are published in the *Guardian*. The situation is a little different in the U.S., where there is no dominant official government model, but a greater number of individual models, whose proprietors regularly prepare forecasts that are the subject of comment and discussion in the financial press. The comparative sizes of five models are presented in the following table, taken from the *Report* of the Committee on Policy Optimisation (1978).

| Model | Number of equations Behavioural | Identities | Total |
|---|---|---|---|
| Treasury | 300 | 283 | 583 |
| London Business School | 156 | 128ˈ | 284 |
| National Institute | 70 | 80 | 150 |
| US Federal Reserve Board | 69 | 125 | 194 |
| Wharton School (Pennsylvania) | 70 | 137 | 207 |

The simple Keynesian model is in itself of little use for empirical work, but substantially developed (often in non-Keynesian ways) lies at the heart of most macroeconometric models. The elementary system represents the markets for goods, money, and labour. The goods market comprises a consumption function, an investment function, and an identity:

$$C = C(Y), I = I(r), Y = C + I,$$

(the identity having been obtained by eliminating savings, $S$, from $Y = C + S$ and $S = I$). From this follows the *IS* curve as a partial reduced form relating income to the rate of interest. A further relation (the *LM* curve) is derived from the liquidity preference function

$$M/P = kY + M_2(r),$$

assuming that the money supply $M$ is exogenously given and equilibrium prevails. The *IS* and *LM* curves intersect at some combination of the interest rate and income, determining $r$ and $Y$ assuming that the price level $P$ is given. The labour market contains a production function giving real output as a function of employment $N$, a marginal productivity condition giving labour demand as a function of the real wage $W/P$, and a labour supply function in terms of the money wage:

$$Y = Y(N), \ W/P = Y'(N), \ W = W_0 + W(N).$$

The whole system has seven equations, and determines the endogenous variables, $C$, $I$, $Y$, $r$, $P$, $N$ and $W$ in terms of the exogenous variable $M$. Most of the basic relations have empirical counterparts in most macroeconometric models, and some of these have been considered in earlier chapters. However a number of extensions are required to make the model useful for empirical work.

First, as it stands the model is entirely static and contains no dynamic behaviour, nor any link between one period and the next. The time period is assumed sufficiently short for capital stock to be taken as given, and the production function has a single argument, labour input. At the simplest level a link between periods can be obtained by letting investment accumulate and entering the resulting capital stock in the production function, and an immediate next step is an accelerator mechanism. More generally, distributed lag mechanisms of the kind discussed in chapter III may be relevant to a number of behavioural equations. Typically the effects of any exogenous shock will not be felt fully until some time has elapsed, and the relation between short-term and long-term effects and the nature of the system's approach to the long-run position are of considerable interest in forecasting models, while longer term growth models are oriented towards the study of the behaviour of equilibrium growth paths.

Secondly, further sectors are required, particularly to model foreign trade and payments and government expenditure and taxes. Of course in U.S. models the foreign sector is relatively smaller than in U.K. models, nevertheless import and export demand functions are typically added. Also in the U.K. an important category is "invisibles", that is, payments on current account for which there is no corresponding physical commodity, examples being insurance and tourist services and interest and dividends on overseas investments. While tax rates and allowances are usually treated as parameters or exogenous variables (policy instruments), tax revenues are typically endogenous since the various tax bases are themselves determined within the model. Once government expenditure and the public sector borrowing requirement enter the model, the role of the financial sector is implicitly recognised. A connection between these two further sectors then arises if, under a floating exchange rate system, fiscal and monetary policy must be associated with exchange rate policy.

Thirdly, disaggregation of the simple Keynesian model is required in various ways. The aggregate expenditure variables already discussed may be broken down into components with different determinants and different speeds of adjustment, for example consumers' expenditure on durables and non-durables might be considered separately, likewise investment in plant and equipment, residential construction, stocks and work-in-progress. Disaggregation of the income variable arises in a variety of ways, since there is no unique definition of income in national accounts. Economic statisticians have been preoccupied to reconcile the three alternative *GDP* definitions – income, output and expenditure – or provide some compromise series. The income approach distinguishes wages and salaries, profits, and dividends, each of which has different determinants and may relate differently to expenditure. In the output approach value added is calculated by industry, which provides a further direction of disaggregation. The expenditure approach $(Y=C+I+G+X-M)$ is implicit in the preceding remarks. Disaggregation over time is a further dimension, proceeding from the early annual models of Tinbergen and Klein to the present-day quarterly models. Of course an annual model might suffice to describe the gross, long-run outcome of economic changes, but the finer description of dynamic reactions provided by quarterly models is important in the analysis and forecasting of business cycle developments. Quarterly models began to be constructed as soon as quarterly national income data over a sufficiently long period became available, the quarterly model of the U.K. economy constructed by Klein *et al.* (1961) being an important step. However, there are still some industrial countries where the requisite data are not available.

In developing the simple macro-model, one guide is provided by economic theory, as we have seen in the discussion of the specification of particular relationships in the preceding chapters. On the other hand the problem to be solved influences the form of the model, and the type of policy objective to be considered influences the level of disaggregation and size of the model. The main reason for the growth of models to the size indicated above is the need to model the channels through which various policy instruments affect the economy, and in practice the number of available instruments is large. The tax system involves a large number of different rates and allowances, and monetary and interest rate policy works through many channels. To the extent that one is interested in the differential impact of particular measures on particular groups or sectors of the economy or particular types of expenditure, a full account of these impacts is required. Of course for some purposes one might simply wish to forecast broad aggregates, in which case a smaller, more aggregated model might suffice. Even here, however, a more detailed specification of the behaviour of particular components of the aggregate, to the extent that they differ, might improve forecasts of the aggregate. In practice it is not clear that large models forecast better than smaller ones, although in such comparisons the fact that the larger model provides information on a number of matters about which the smaller model has nothing to say is usually neglected, and an emphasis on forecast performance distorts the appraisal of alternative models that serve different ends.

In the construction of large-scale economy-wide models an alternative approach is provided by the Cambridge Growth Project model: see Barker (1976) and references to earlier work contained therein. The model is designed to investigate structural change in the economy, and so is a multisectoral model. It is an annual model projecting over the medium term of 4-6 years in the future to allow time for the structure to change, and abstracting from the short-term, transient effects of economic policy. A central feature of the model, and a key distinction from the statistical macroeconometric models mentioned above, is an input-output table showing the input of 45 commodities per unit of output of 35 industries. The motivation is that the demand by domestic industries for inputs of materials and services is the largest component of total demand, which must be modelled if the structural effects of final demand on industrial output and employment are to be studied.

### FORECASTING, DYNAMIC MULTIPLIERS AND POLICY ANALYSIS

In this section we consider forecasting and dynamic analysis with a *linear* simultaneous equation model, reserving the generalisation to non-linear models until later. The model describes the relations between the elements of a vector of current endogenous variables $y_t$ and a vector of predetermined (exogenous and lagged endogenous) variables $z_t$ together with disturbances $u_t$, and is written in *structural form* as

$$By_t + \Gamma z_t = u_t.$$

Estimates of the structural parameters $B$ and $\Gamma$ provide information about elasticities, marginal propensities, reaction coefficients, and so forth. Identities are distinguished as equations in which the numerical values of the parameters are known and the disturbance term is identically zero. The contemporaneous feedbacks between endogenous variables are solved out in the *reduced form*

$$y_t = \Pi z_t + v_t, \; \Pi = -B^{-1} \Gamma, \; v_t = B^{-1} u_t \, ,$$

and these reduced form equations can be used to forecast the endogenous variables one-at-a-time. Having obtained estimates $\hat{B}$, $\hat{\Gamma}$ of the structural parameters, the reduced form coefficient estimates are calculated as $\hat{\Pi} = -\hat{B}^{-1} \hat{\Gamma}$, and if the disturbances are non-autocorrelated so that the best forecasts of them are given by their mean values, namely zero, the forecasting equations are of the form

$$y_t = \hat{\Pi} z_t.$$

Note that solving for the reduced form coefficient estimates in this way should be distinguished from direct estimation of $\Pi$ by multivariate multiple regression, that is, by regressing in turn each element of $y_t$ on the predetermined variables $z_t$. Most systems are overidentified and there are a large number of zeros in the $\hat{B}$ and $\hat{\Gamma}$ matrices as a result of the theoretical specification. These restrictions are incorporated in the reduced form equations deduced from the structure. The forecasting equations then obey the restrictions imposed upon the model, a property which does not hold for the reduced form equations obtained by direct regression. The only prior information incorporated in the directly estimated reduced form is the categorisation of variables as endogenous or exogenous. The argument for preferring the "solved out" forecasting equations is simply that they will forecast better if the *a priori* restrictions are correct, being based on more information.

We distinguish ex-ante and ex-post predictions. The former conform to the usual forecasting or future prediction exercise where it is also necessary to project predetermined variables during the forecasting period. Suppose we have a sample period $t = 1, \ldots, T$, and a forecast period $t = T+1, T+2, \ldots$ Then using projections of the $z_{T+j}$ variables or information about their likely future behaviour, the ex-ante forecasts are given by

$$\hat{y}_{T+j} = \hat{\Pi}\hat{z}_{T+j} \qquad j = 1, 2, \ldots$$

In comparing forecasts $\hat{y}_{T+j}$ with the actual values assumed to have been generated by

$$y_{T+j} = \Pi z_{T+j} + v_{T+j}$$

in the absence of specification error, we may distinguish three possible sources of error. The first arises from the disturbance term in the reduced form equation. This is set equal to zero for forecasting purposes but the actual value of $v_{T+j}$ will differ from its expected value. Secondly, the coefficient estimates $\hat{\Pi}$ will differ from the true values $\Pi$ — there will be sampling errors due to sample period disturbance terms. Thirdly, we may have information errors — errors in the predictions of the values of $z_{T+j}$. These three contributions to ex-ante forecast error can be noted (in reverse order) by writing

$$y_{T+j} - \hat{y}_{T+j} = \Pi z_{T+j} + v_{T+j} - \hat{\Pi}\hat{z}_{T+j}$$

$$= \hat{\Pi}(z_{T+j} - \hat{z}_{T+j}) - (\hat{\Pi} - \Pi)z_{T+j} + v_{T+j}.$$

Information error can be eliminated when the forecasting performance is examined after the event, by using the actual realised values of $z_{T+j}$. This is what happens in ex-post forecasting, where we use the estimated coefficients but the true $z_{T+j}$:

$$\tilde{y}_{T+j} = \hat{\Pi} z_{T+j} .$$

Ex-post forecasts can of course be obtained within the sample period ($\tilde{y}_t = \hat{\Pi} z_t$, $t=1, \ldots, T$), which is implicit in the calculation of $R^2$ for a single regression equation, this being based on $\tilde{y}_t$ and $y_t$ over the estimation period. Thus ex-post forecasts might be more appropriately termed backcasts! The two sources of forecast error are given by

$$y_{T+j} - \tilde{y}_{T+j} = v_{T+j} - (\hat{\Pi} - \Pi) z_{T+j}.$$

While it is often said that the crucial test of a model is an examination of its predictive performance outside the sample period, the use of ex-post forecasts is more relevant in such a test, since they emphasise the properties of the model and abstract from the forecasting of exogenous variables, which by definition takes place outside the model. Estimates of the variance of ex-post forecast errors can be calculated from the sample data, being based on the estimated variances of the coefficients and disturbances. If a particular set of forecast errors appears to be substantially greater than would be expected on these grounds, then we would conclude that the estimated model does not adequately represent the real world in the forecast period, and that the data no longer provide support for the original specification of the structure: formal tests are available for this purpose. Whether a particular structural change can be identified as the cause of the discrepancy, or whether a particular behavioural hypothesis can be blamed, is then a matter for detailed examination of the predictions of the separate variables. However note that such tests are not very powerful, since a specification error may have an equal effect on the sample-period and forecast-period behaviour of the model. For example, omitting a relevant variable increases the residual variance of an equation and biases its coefficients, but it is not necessarily the case that forecasts from the misspecified equation will have mean squared error greater than that anticipated on the basis of (erroneous) sample-period calculations, nor that the forecast-period mean squared error will be any different from the sample-period mean squared error: if the behaviour of the variables is unchanged, the forecast-period estimates will be just as wrong as the sample-period estimates! Crucial differences arise when the behaviour of variables changes, and the example discussed at the end of chapter I might be seen in this light: inflation effects should have been included in the consumption function, but this only became apparent when the behaviour of the inflation series changed.

To extend the forecast formulae to dynamic models, when further possibilities arise, we distinguish between exogenous variables and lagged endogenous variables, considering in the present section the case of one-period lags. Partitioning the vector $z_t$ into a vector of purely exogenous variables (current or lagged) $x_t$ and the lagged endogenous variables $y_{t-1}$, and partitioning the reduced form coefficient matrix to conform we write the reduced form as

$$y_t = \Pi_1 y_{t-1} + \Pi_2 x_t + v_t.$$

The matrix $\Pi_1$ is square, but if a particular endogenous variable does not appear lagged in any equation of the model then the corresponding column of $\Pi_1$ is zero, which has the effect of excluding that element of $y_{t-1}$ from the reduced form. In ex-ante forecasting one period ahead, information error is now restricted to the exogenous variables, since forecasts for next period embody the value of the lagged endogenous variables in that period, but these are simply the (known) current values of the endogenous variables. So such forecasts are given by

$$\hat{y}_{T+1} = \hat{\Pi}_1 y_T + \hat{\Pi}_2 \hat{x}_{T+1}.$$

Then, in calculating a sequence of forecasts of increasing horizon as of period $T$, the forecast for one period enters into the calculation of the next:

$$\hat{y}_{T+j} = \hat{\Pi}_1 \hat{y}_{T+j-1} + \hat{\Pi}_2 \hat{x}_{T+j}, \quad j = 2,3,\ldots$$

Ex-post all the predetermined variables are known and we can treat the lagged endogenous variables in one of two ways. We may either use the actual values or, as above, allow the model to generate a sequence of forecasts as a function of initial conditions, the forecasts sequentially generating their own lagged values as follows:

$$\bar{y}_{T+1} = \hat{\Pi}_1 y_T + \hat{\Pi}_2 x_{T+1}$$

$$\bar{y}_{T+j} = \hat{\Pi}_1 \bar{y}_{T+j-1} + \hat{\Pi}_2 x_{T+j}, j = 2,3,\ldots$$

This latter possibility is more relevant to the study of how the system reflects the dynamic behaviour of the economy over a number of periods, to which we now turn.

In considering the dynamic properties of the model, whether we are working with estimated coefficients or true parameter values is of little consequence for the analysis, so we simplify by dropping hats, also leave the error term aside, and consider the system

$$y_t = \Pi_1 y_{t-1} + \Pi_2 x_t.$$

The coefficients in the matrix $\Pi_2$ give the immediate change in the endogenous variables in response to a unit change in an exogenous variable — the *impact multipliers*. Subsequently a maintained change or step in an exogenous variable beginning at time $t$ has continuing effects which work through the system as follows:

$$y_t = \Pi_1 y_{t-1} + \Pi_2 x_t$$

$$y_{t+1} = \Pi_1 y_t + \Pi_2 x_{t+1} = \Pi_1^2 y_{t-1} + \Pi_1 \Pi_2 x_t + \Pi_2 x_{t+1}$$

$$y_{t+2} = \Pi_1 y_{t+1} + \Pi_2 x_{t+2} = \Pi_1^3 y_{t-1} + \Pi_1^2 \Pi_2 x_t + \Pi_1 \Pi_2 x_{t+1} + \Pi_2 x_{t+2}$$

and so on. Thus, whereas the impact multipliers are given by $\Pi_2$, the various *dynamic multipliers* are given by

$$\Pi_2 + \Pi_1 \Pi_2 \qquad \text{for the effect after one period}$$

$$(I + \Pi_1 + \Pi_1^2)\Pi_2 \qquad \text{for the effect after two periods}$$

$$\vdots \qquad\qquad \vdots$$

$$(I + \Pi_1 + \ldots + \Pi_1^j)\Pi_2 \qquad \text{for the effect after } j \text{ periods.}$$

If the matrix $\Pi_1$ is such that $\Pi_1^j$ tends to a zero matrix as $j \to \infty$, then the total or long-run effect is given by

$$\sum_{j=0}^{\infty} \Pi_1^j \Pi_2 = (I - \Pi_1)^{-1}\Pi_2.$$

These quantities are called *equilibrium multipliers* by Goldberger (1959), and are the matrix generalisation of the long-run multipliers discussed in chapter I. That is, the relation between the static equilibrium values is given by solving

$$y^e = \Pi_1 y^e + \Pi_2 x^e$$

to obtain

$$y^e = (I - \Pi_1)^{-1} \Pi_2 x^e.$$

The $(g,k)$ element of this matrix describes the change in the equilibrium or long-run level of the endogenous variable $y_g$ in response to a unit change in the exogenous variable $x_k$. The condition for $\Pi_1^j$ to converge to zero as $j$ increases is that all the eigenvalues of the matrix $\Pi_1$ have modulus less than 1, and this provides a stability condition for the model (cf. Glaister, 1978, Ch. 9). The nature of these eigenvalues determines the speed of approach to equilibrium, and whether this approach is smooth or oscillatory. In practice, the corresponding eigenvalues calculated from estimated coefficients provide useful information about the adequacy of the dynamic specification of the model; in particular, if a calculated eigenvalue is substantially greater than 1 while the underlying actual situation is essentially stable, the estimated model cannot be accepted as a realistic representation.

If this stability condition is satisfied then by repeated substitution for the lagged endogenous variables we obtain

$$y_t = \Pi_2 x_t + \Pi_1 \Pi_2 x_{t-1} + \Pi_1^2 \Pi_2 x_{t-2} + \ldots$$

$$= \sum_{j=0}^{\infty} \Pi_1^{\,j} \Pi_2 x_{t-j}.$$

This representation gives each current endogenous variable as a function of the infinite past of the exogenous variables, and is termed the *final form*. Elements of the matrices $\Pi_1^{\,j} \Pi_2$ give the effect of a unit shock (not sustained) in an exogenous variable on an endogenous variable $j$ periods later. Theil and Boot (1962) term these "interim multipliers": they are the matrix generalisation of distributed lag reaction coefficients. Indeed, the above equation is the matrix generalisation of the geometric distributed lag, and the return from this form to the reduced form is a generalisation of the Koyck transformation.

Dynamic multipliers describe the effects over time of an exogenous variable used as a policy instrument. Since we have a linear model, the effect of a policy package can be evaluated by combining the appropriate dynamic or equilibrium multipliers. Suits (1962, §1) presents some simple examples in the context of an illustrative four-equation model. For instance, an increase in government spending is combined with an increase in the tax schedule (via its intercept term). Such a policy package may be described as an ex-ante balanced budget policy, for both government income and expenditure are increased by the same amount, and corresponding balanced budget multipliers can be calculated. Ex-post, however, the policy yields a surplus, for while the increase in government expenditure is balanced by the increased tax yield at the original level of income, the policy itself changes income and hence the tax yield, which no longer exactly balances the budget. Since the effect of government expenditure on income is greater than that of taxation, income and hence the tax yield increase, giving an ex-post budget surplus.

## AN ILLUSTRATION: KLEIN MODEL I

As an example of an estimated model, we present the six-equation Keynesian income-expenditure model of the U.S. economy, 1921-1941, by Klein (1950), known as Klein's Model I. Although very much on the small side by current standards, it will serve to illustrate the analysis without obscuring it in a more detailed specification. Over the years, the model has also been used as a test-bed for virtually every new technique of estimation and analysis that has been introduced.

The consumption function allows differing propensities to consume for different components or classes of income, so aggregate consumption $(C)$ is a function of profits $(P)$ current and lagged, and the sum of the wage bill in private industry $(W_1)$ and government $(W_2)$:

$$C = 16.79 + 0.020\,P + 0.235\,P_{-1} + 0.800\,(W_1 + W_2) + \hat{u}_1.$$

A profits theory of investment is adopted, so net investment $(I)$ is given in terms of current and lagged profits, and beginning-year capital stock $(K_{-1})$:

$$I = 17.78 + 0.231\,P + 0.546\,P_{-1} - 0.146\,K_{-1} + \hat{u}_2.$$

A labour demand equation follows, giving the private wage bill as a function of net national income $(Y)$ plus business taxes $(T)$ less the government wage bill, all current and lagged, together with a time trend (measured in calendar years)

$$W_1 = 1.60 + 0.420\,(Y{+}T{-}W_2) + 0.164\,(Y{+}T{-}W_2)_{-1}$$

$$+ 0.135\,(t{-}1935) + \hat{u}_3.$$

Then follow three identities, namely the expenditure and income definitions of national income, and the definition of net investment:

$$Y + T = C + I + G$$
$$Y = W_1 + W_2 + P$$
$$I = K - K_{-1}.$$

The endogenous variables are $C$, $I$, $W_1$, $Y$, $P$, and $K$, and there are four exogenous variables: $W_2$, $T$, $G$, and $t$. Adding lagged variables, the total number of predetermined variables appearing in the model is nine. Thus each of the first three equations is over-identified, and the estimates reported above are obtained by the method of full-information maximum likelihood, which estimates the whole model simultaneously, taking all the restrictions into account.

In presenting the reduced form, we re-order the endogenous variables so that the zero columns of the matrix $\Pi_1$, corresponding to variables whose lagged values do not appear, are the last three columns. The reduced form coefficients, given by Theil and Boot (1962), are as follows:

$$
\begin{bmatrix} P \\ Y \\ K \\ C \\ W_1 \\ I \end{bmatrix}
=
\begin{bmatrix}
0.863 & -0.063 & -0.164 & 0 & 0 & 0 \\
1.489 & 0.174 & -0.283 & 0 & 0 & 0 \\
0.746 & -0.015 & 0.816 & 0 & 0 & 0 \\
0.743 & 0.189 & -0.098 & 0 & 0 & 0 \\
0.626 & 0.237 & -0.119 & 0 & 0 & 0 \\
0.746 & -0.015 & -0.184 & 0 & 0 & 0
\end{bmatrix}
\begin{bmatrix} P \\ Y \\ K \\ C \\ W_1 \\ I \end{bmatrix}_{-1}
$$

$$
+
\begin{bmatrix}
-0.224 & -1.281 & 1.119 & -0.052 & 0.063 & -0.063 \\
0.614 & -1.484 & 1.930 & 0.143 & -0.174 & 0.174 \\
-0.052 & -0.296 & 0.259 & -0.012 & 0.015 & -0.015 \\
0.666 & -0.188 & 0.671 & 0.155 & -0.189 & 0.189 \\
-0.162 & -0.204 & 0.811 & 0.195 & -0.237 & 0.237 \\
-0.052 & -0.296 & 0.259 & -0.012 & 0.015 & -0.015
\end{bmatrix}
\begin{bmatrix} W_2 \\ T \\ G \\ t \\ (W_2)_{-1} \\ T_{-1} \end{bmatrix}
$$

Thus a billion dollar increase in government expenditure increases consumption in the current period by 0.671 billions, and the ex-ante balanced budget income multiplier is $1.930 - 1.484 = 0.446$. Theil and Boot go on to calculate interim multipliers $\Pi_1{}^j\Pi_2$: changes in sign occur, the system exhibiting damped oscillations as it returns to equilibrium. (Note that some care is needed in the treatment of lagged exogenous variables in these calculations. Note also that the term "final equation", which following Tinbergen (1939) we have used to denote an equation relating an endogenous variable to its own lagged values and exogenous variables, is used by Theil and Boot for what has been defined above as the final form.) Total multipliers $(I - \Pi_1)^{-1}\Pi_2$ are also presented for maintained changes in three of the exogenous variables as follows:

|       | $P$    | $Y$    | $K$    | $C$    | $W_1$   | $I$ |
|-------|--------|--------|--------|--------|---------|-----|
| $W_2$ | −0.192 | 0.536  | −1.024 | 0.536  | −0.271  | 0   |
| $T$   | −1.237 | −1.569 | −6.564 | −0.569 | −0.333  | 0   |
| $G$   | 0.965  | 2.323  | 5.123  | 1.323  | 1.358   | 0   |

Thus the ex-ante balanced budget income multiplier in the long run is $2.323 - 1.569 = 0.754$, and so about three-fifths of the long run effect occurs in the first year.

Finally, the question of stability can be investigated by calculating the eigenvalues of $\Pi_1$. Of course, having already observed that the interim multipliers die away as $j$ increases, we expect to find that the eigenvalues have modulus less than 1. Since $\Pi_1$ has three zero columns, there are only three non-zero eigenvalues, and these are obtained as the eigenvalues of the 3X3 submatrix in the top left-hand corner. The latent roots given by Theil and Boot comprise one real root and a pair of complex conjugate roots:

$$\lambda_1, \lambda_2 = 0.838 \; (\cos 0.435 \pm i \sin 0.435)$$

$$\lambda_3 = 0.334.$$

Clearly, these roots have modulus less than 1, so the system is stable though oscillatory.

Following this illustration of the methods of analysis for linear systems with one-period lagged endogenous variables, in the next three sections we consider the relaxation of three of the simplifying assumptions that have been made. First, we consider higher order dynamic systems, next non-linear models and then we reintroduce the disturbance term.

## GENERAL DYNAMIC MODELS

We retain the assumption of linearity, but now allow endogenous variables to appear with a lag of more than one period. Assuming that the maximum lag in any endogenous variable is of $r$ periods, we write the model in *structural form* as follows:

$$\mathbf{B}_0 \mathbf{y}_t + \mathbf{B}_1 \mathbf{y}_{t-1} + \ldots + \mathbf{B}_r \mathbf{y}_{t-r} + \Gamma \mathbf{x}_t = \mathbf{u}_t.$$

It is convenient in the following analysis to use $\beta$'s to denote the coefficients of endogenous variables, current or lagged, and to redefine $\Gamma$ as the matrix of coefficients of the purely exogenous variables. The $\mathbf{B}_l$ matrices are all square, and if a particular $y$-variable does not appear with a given lag, say $l$ periods, anywhere in the model, then the corresponding column of $\mathbf{B}_l$ is zero. In practice we might expect only a few variables to appear with the maximum lag $r$ in relatively few equations, so that the higher order coefficient matrices are typically rather sparse. Denoting the number of endogenous variables (and equations) by $G$ and the number of exogenous variables by $K$, an ordinary algebraic representation of a typical equation, the $g$th, is

$$\sum_{i=1}^{G} \sum_{l=0}^{r} \beta_{gil} y_{i,t-l} + \sum_{k=1}^{K} \gamma_{gk} x_{kt} = u_{gt}, \quad g = 1, \ldots, G.$$

The *reduced form* in effect recombines lagged endogenous and exogenous variables, being given by

$$\mathbf{y}_t = - \mathbf{B}_0^{-1} (\mathbf{B}_1 \mathbf{y}_{t-1} + \ldots + \mathbf{B}_r \mathbf{y}_{t-r} + \Gamma \mathbf{x}_t) + \mathbf{B}_0^{-1} \mathbf{u}_t .$$

If $r=1$ we have the simple first-order dynamic system again, and then the matrix $-\mathbf{B}_0^{-1} \mathbf{B}_1$ is what was previously denoted by $\Pi_1$. In general each reduced form equation expresses an endogenous variable as a function of predetermined variables and error terms, and the autocorrelation properties of the reduced form error terms are the same as those of the structural disturbances: if the $u$'s are non-autocorrelated, so are the reduced form errors. These equations are useful in forecasting exercises, but for dynamic analysis this is not the most useful solution form, since in order to study the behaviour over time of a particular endogenous variable it is necessary to consider the complete system, as all other endogenous variables appear lagged on the right-hand side.

To obtain alternative solution forms, it is convenient to introduce $\mathbf{B}(L)$, defined by

$$\mathbf{B}(L) = \mathbf{B}_0 + \mathbf{B}_1 L + \ldots + \mathbf{B}_r L^r ,$$

a matrix whose elements are polynomials in the lag operator L. $\mathbf{B}(L)$ has $(g,i)$ element

$$\sum_{l=0}^{r} \beta_{gil} L^l.$$

The model now is

$$\mathbf{B}(L) \, \mathbf{y}_t = - \, \Gamma \mathbf{x}_t + \mathbf{u}_t$$

and the *final form* solution is

$$\mathbf{y}_t = - \, \mathbf{B}(L)^{-1} \, \Gamma \mathbf{x}_t + \mathbf{B}(L)^{-1} \mathbf{u}_t.$$

Here each endogenous variable is expressed as an infinite distributed lag function of exogenous variables, together with an error term comprising moving averages of the original disturbances. The coefficients in the expansion of $-\mathbf{B}(L)^{-1} \, \Gamma$ are the interim multipliers describing the response of $y_{it}$ to a unit shock in $x_{k,t-l}$. In empirical work the infinite distributed lag would generally be replaced by a rational approximation, but in the present context an explicit expression is obtained by recalling that the inverse of a matrix is given by the adjoint matrix divided by the determinant (scalar), so we can write

$$\mathbf{B}(L)^{-1} = \frac{\mathbf{b}(L)}{|\mathbf{B}(L)|},$$

where $\mathbf{b}(L)$ is the adjoint matrix of $\mathbf{B}(L)$ and $|\mathbf{B}(L)|$ the determinant.

Substituting this in the preceding equation and multiplying through by $|\mathbf{B}(L)|$ gives

$$|\mathbf{B}(L)|y_t = - \mathbf{b}(L) \, \Gamma x_t + \mathbf{b}(L)u_t \, .$$

These are the *final equations* of Tinbergen (1939) and Goldberger (1959). Each equation relates a given endogenous variable to its own past values and to the exogenous variables at various points in time, but to no other endogenous variable, current or lagged. Thus to study the time path of an endogenous variable in terms of the time paths of the exogenous variables, a single final equation is all that is required. The important characteristics are

(i) each final equation has the same autoregressive structure, given by the polynomial $|\mathbf{B}(L)|$, which is of degree $\leq Gr$,

(ii) finite lags in exogenous variables appear, generally different between equations,

(iii) the error terms are moving averages of the structural disturbance terms, again generally different between equations.

Thus an assessment of the stability of the model requires an examination of only one final equation, since they all have the same autoregressive structure; in particular an examination of $|\mathbf{B}(L)|$ is required. The degree of this polynomial in L will generally be considerably less than $Gr$, for this only obtains if all variables appear with an $r$-period lag each in a different equation, that is, if $\mathbf{B}_r$ is non-singular. The polynomial can be factorised into a product of factors $(1 - c_iL)$, and the stability condition is that the coefficients $c_i$ have modulus less than 1 (cf. pp.94-95 and Glaister, 1978, Ch. 9). This is equivalent to the condition that the "characteristic equation"

$$|\mathbf{B}_0z^r + \mathbf{B}_1z^{r-1} + \ldots + \mathbf{B}_{r-1} z + \mathbf{B}_r| = 0$$

has roots with modulus less than 1.

*Example 1: multiplier-accelerator models*

An illustration is provided by the following simple national income model:

$$C_t = \alpha + \beta Y_t + u_{1t}$$

$$Y_t = C_t + I_t + G_t$$

$$I_t = \gamma(Y_t - Y_{t-1}) + u_{2t}.$$

This can be written in the present format as follows

$$
\begin{bmatrix} 1 & -\beta & 0 \\ -1 & 1 & -1 \\ 0 & -\gamma(1-L) & 1 \end{bmatrix}
\begin{bmatrix} C_t \\ Y_t \\ I_t \end{bmatrix}
=
\begin{bmatrix} \alpha & 0 \\ 0 & 1 \\ 0 & 0 \end{bmatrix}
\begin{bmatrix} 1 \\ G_t \end{bmatrix}
+
\begin{bmatrix} u_{1t} \\ 0 \\ u_{2t} \end{bmatrix}
$$

Here $r=1$, $\mathbf{B}_1$ has only one non-zero element, and the determinant of $\mathbf{B}(L)$ is $1-\gamma(1-L)-\beta$. For convenience we combine the right-hand side terms into a column vector with elements $\alpha+u_{1t}$, $G_t$, $u_{2t}$. Then, entering the adjoint matrix on the right-hand side, we have the final equations

$$
(1-\beta-\gamma+\gamma L)
\begin{bmatrix} C_t \\ Y_t \\ I_t \end{bmatrix}
=
\begin{bmatrix} 1-\gamma(1-L) & \beta & \beta \\ 1 & 1 & 1 \\ \gamma(1-L) & \gamma(1-L) & 1-\beta \end{bmatrix}
\begin{bmatrix} \alpha+u_{1t} \\ G_t \\ u_{2t} \end{bmatrix}.
$$

If each final equation is written out with the lagged dependent variable on the right-hand side, then we see that in each case there is one lagged value, with coefficient $-\gamma/(1-\beta-\gamma)$: the stability condition is that this coefficient is less than 1 in absolute value, and it is immaterial which final equation we look at. A lagged value of the exogenous variable is introduced only into the third final equation, and the first and third equations have error terms involving current and lagged values of $u_1$ and so will in general be autocorrelated even if $u_1$ is non-autocorrelated. The characteristic equation

$$|\mathbf{B}_0 z + \mathbf{B}_1| = 0$$

has root

$$z = \frac{-\gamma}{1-\beta-\gamma},$$

giving the same stability condition as above.

This model is a simple version of the Hicks-Samuelson multiplier-accelerator model, that discussed by Samuelson (1939) being as follows:

$$C_t = \alpha + \beta Y_{t-1} + u_{1t}$$

$$Y_t = C_t + I_t + G_t$$

$$I_t = \gamma(Y_{t-1} - Y_{t-2}) + u_{2t}.$$

For this model we have

$$\mathbf{B}(L) = \begin{bmatrix} 1 & -\beta L & 0 \\ -1 & 1 & -1 \\ 0 & -\gamma L(1-L) & 1 \end{bmatrix},$$

$$|\mathbf{B}(L)| = 1 - (\gamma+\beta)L + \gamma L^2,$$

so the final equations are second-order autoregressions. Stability requires that the roots of

$$z^2 - (\gamma+\beta)z + \gamma = 0$$

have modulus less than 1, and since the product of the roots is $\gamma$, we see that with the usual interpretation of $\gamma$ as the capital-output ratio the model is unstable.

*Example 2: a wage-price model*

An empirical example of stability analysis carried out via the characteristic equation is provided by Thomas and Stoney (1970), who examine the dynamic properties of the three-equation wage-price model of Hines (1964). The endogenous variables are the rates of change of wage rates and retail prices, and the percentage of the labour force unionized. One-period lagged values of these variables appear in the model in such a way that the characteristic equation is of second degree. Using Hines' 2SLS estimated coefficients, Thomas and Stoney find that the roots of the characteristic equation are 0.797 and 7.21, the latter value suggesting that the model is dynamically unstable. However, Thomas and Stoney argue that some of Hines' rate of change variables are inappropriately defined, particularly insofar as the timing relationships between variables are concerned, and accordingly modify the method of calculating the rate of change of prices. The resulting model, with these small changes in dynamic specification, has a third-degree characteristic equation with roots −0.88, 0.76, and 0.61, and the standard errors are such that these are all significantly below unity. Thus they conclude that "while Hines' estimated three equation model is dynamically unstable, it is possible to remove this instability by appropriately redefining the price variable". The study demonstrates the value ·of an examination of the stability implications of an estimated dynamic system as a validation procedure for that system.

An alternative approach is to write the reduced form of $G$ $r$th-order difference equations as a first order difference equation in an augmented y-vector, as follows (cf. Glaister, 1978, Ch. 9):

$$
\begin{bmatrix} y_t \\ y_{t-1} \\ y_{t-2} \\ \vdots \\ y_{t-r+1} \end{bmatrix} = \begin{bmatrix} -B_0^{-1} B_1 & -B_0^{-1} B_2 & \cdots & -B_0^{-1} B_r \\ I & 0 & \cdots & 0 \\ 0 & I & \cdots & 0 \\ \vdots & \vdots & & \vdots \\ 0 & 0 & \cdots I & 0 \end{bmatrix} \begin{bmatrix} y_{t-1} \\ y_{t-2} \\ y_{t-3} \\ \vdots \\ y_{t-r} \end{bmatrix}
$$

$$
+ \begin{bmatrix} -B_0^{-1} \Gamma \\ 0 \\ \vdots \\ 0 \end{bmatrix} x_t + \begin{bmatrix} B_0^{-1} \\ 0 \\ \vdots \\ 0 \end{bmatrix} u_t.
$$

Denoting the $Gr$-element vector on the left-hand side by $y_t^*$, and the $Gr \times Gr$ matrix of coefficients by $\mathbf{A}$, we now have a vector first order difference equation

$$y_t^* = \mathbf{A}y_{t-1}^* + \Pi_2^* x_t + v_t^*.$$

Thus in practice we need only consider first order systems, as a result of this device, and the matrix $\mathbf{A}$ takes the place of the matrix $\Pi_1$ introduced on p.135. Again the stability condition is that the eigenvalues of $\mathbf{A}$ have modulus less than 1. These eigenvalues or latent roots are obtained as the solutions of the determinantal equation

$$\begin{vmatrix} -\mathbf{B}_0^{-1}\mathbf{B}_1 - \lambda\mathbf{I} & -\mathbf{B}_0^{-1}\mathbf{B}_2 & -\mathbf{B}_0^{-1}\mathbf{B}_3 & \cdots & -\mathbf{B}_0^{-1}\mathbf{B}_r \\ \mathbf{I} & -\lambda\mathbf{I} & 0 & \cdots & 0 \\ 0 & \mathbf{I} & -\lambda\mathbf{I} & \cdots & 0 \\ \vdots & \vdots & \vdots & & \vdots \\ 0 & 0 & 0 & \cdots \ \mathbf{I} & -\lambda\mathbf{I} \end{vmatrix} = 0$$

Expanding, and assuming that $r$ is even for convenience, this becomes

$$|\lambda^r \mathbf{I} + \mathbf{B}_0^{-1}\mathbf{B}_1\lambda^{r-1}\mathbf{I} + \mathbf{B}_0^{-1}\mathbf{B}_2\lambda^{r-2}\mathbf{I} + \ldots$$

$$+ \mathbf{B}_0^{-1}\mathbf{B}_{r-1}\lambda\mathbf{I} + \mathbf{B}_0^{-1}\mathbf{B}_r| = 0.$$

Multiplying through by $|\mathbf{B}_0|$ gives

$$|\mathbf{B}_0\lambda^r + \mathbf{B}_1\lambda^{r-1} + \mathbf{B}_2\lambda^{r-2} + \ldots + \mathbf{B}_{r-1}\lambda + \mathbf{B}_r| = 0,$$

so the stability condition is exactly as derived above. In general the number of non-zero eigenvalues will be less than the maximum possible, $Gr$. Note that this approach requires the calculation of the reduced form, whereas in the former approach the structural parameters were used directly.

*Example 1 again*

The Samuelson model has

$$\mathbf{B}_0 = \begin{bmatrix} 1 & 0 & 0 \\ -1 & 1 & -1 \\ 0 & 0 & 1 \end{bmatrix}, \text{ so } \mathbf{B}_0^{-1} = \begin{bmatrix} 1 & 0 & 0 \\ 1 & 1 & 1 \\ 0 & 0 & 1 \end{bmatrix},$$

and with $\mathbf{y}_t^* = (C_t, Y_t, I_t, C_{t-1}, Y_{t-1}, I_{t-1})'$, the coefficient matrix in the augmented first order system is

$$\mathbf{A} = \begin{bmatrix} 0 & \beta & 0 & 0 & 0 & 0 \\ 0 & \beta{+}\gamma & 0 & 0 & -\gamma & 0 \\ 0 & \gamma & 0 & 0 & -\gamma & 0 \\ 1 & 0 & 0 & 0 & 0 & 0 \\ 0 & 1 & 0 & 0 & 0 & 0 \\ 0 & 0 & 1 & 0 & 0 & 0 \end{bmatrix}.$$

To obtain the eigenvalues we compute

$$|\mathbf{A} - \lambda\mathbf{I}| = \lambda^4 \left\{ \lambda^2 - \lambda(\beta{+}\gamma) + \gamma \right\},$$

hence the stability condition is as obtained earlier.

## NON-LINEAR MODELS

We now consider relaxing the assumption that the model under consideration is linear. In practice, difficulties arise because different functions of some of the variables appear in the model. For example accounting identities might be expressed in current money values, while some behavioural equations contain the corresponding real variables, and perhaps relative prices, thus in one equation we have a variable that is a product or ratio of other variables of the model. Similarly the use of a Cobb-Douglas production function implies the appearance of the logarithms of certain variables, which might appear elsewhere in their original linear form.

Assuming that the random disturbance term is additive, a general representation is given by writing the $i$th equation as

$$f_i(\mathbf{y}_t, \mathbf{z}_t, \theta_i) = u_{it}$$

where $f_i$ is a general function and $\theta_i$ a vector of parameters. This is more general than is required for the common situation of equations that are non-linear in variables but linear in parameters, for which estimation methods such as 2SLS can be employed. For example, suppose that the $i$th equation is of the form

$$y_{it} = \sum_j \beta_{ij} h_{jt} + \sum_k \gamma_{ik} z_{kt} + u_{it}$$

where $h_{jt} = h_j(\mathbf{y}_t, \mathbf{z}_t)$ are general functions of endogenous and predetermined variables. Any functions depending only on predetermined variables can be defined as new predetermined variables and treated as usual. Functions containing endogenous variables that appear elsewhere in the system in their original linear form are treated as new endogenous variables, and estimation can proceed by instrumental variable methods, for example. However, this approach does not extend to systems estimators such as FIML and 3SLS, nor to the analyses based on the reduced form discussed previously.

Given that the structural form is non-linear in variables, solving for the reduced form by linear methods is no longer possible. Nor is the above approach of defining new variables of assistance. For example, a model might contain variables $y_1$, $y_2$ and their ratio $y_1/y_2$: if we attempt to treat the ratio as a separate variable, adding the definition $y_{G+1} = y_1/y_2$, the reduced form expressions are not in general internally consistent. Suppose that there is a single predetermined variable, so that the reduced form forecasting equations are $\hat{y}_{it} = \hat{\pi}_{i0} + \hat{\pi}_{i1} z_t$: in general it will not be true that $\hat{\pi}_{G+1,0} + \hat{\pi}_{G+1,1} z_t = (\hat{\pi}_{10} + \hat{\pi}_{11} z_t)/(\hat{\pi}_{20} + \hat{\pi}_{21} z_t)$. In this situation, solution of the system

$$f_i(\mathbf{y}_t, \mathbf{z}_t, \hat{\theta}_i) = 0, \qquad i = 1, \ldots, G$$

for the values $\mathbf{y}_t$ corresponding to given values of the predetermined variables $\mathbf{z}_t$ proceeds by numerical methods. That is, given the coefficient estimates and projected values for the $z$-variables, the computer seeks, by iterative methods, values for the endogenous variables which satisfy the above equations to the desired degree of accuracy. In practice we do not obtain exactly zero on the right-hand side, but we instruct the computer to keep "improving" the solution values for the endogenous variables until the right-hand side is less than some very small preassigned number.

The amount of computation required can be substantially reduced if the model can be set out in recursive blocks. In a recursive model the matrix of coefficients of the endogenous variables is triangular; in a block-recursive model, the matrix is block-triangular. In the present non-linear situation, assume as an illustration that there are two blocks, so that the problem can be written

$$f_i(\mathbf{y}_{1t}, \mathbf{z}_t, \hat{\theta}_i) = 0, \qquad i = 1, \ldots, G_1$$

$$f_i(\mathbf{y}_{2t}, \mathbf{y}_{1t}, \mathbf{z}_t, \hat{\theta}_i) = 0, \qquad i = G_1 + 1, \ldots, G$$

The vector $\mathbf{y}_t$ is partitioned into sub-vectors $\mathbf{y}_{1t}$ and $\mathbf{y}_{2t}$, and the $G_1$ elements of $\mathbf{y}_{1t}$ are determined in the first block of equations: there is no feedback from $\mathbf{y}_{2t}$ to $\mathbf{y}_{1t}$. These solution values for the first sub-vector can then be regarded as predetermined when the second block of equations is solved for $\mathbf{y}_{2t}$. Thus one large problem becomes two small ones. Note that this structure is not being used to justify block-by-block estimation methods, for in a genuine block-recursive model the errors in different blocks are mutually uncorrelated, but simply to ease the computational burden of obtaining solutions for the endogenous variables in the presence of non-linearities. In practice, seeing whether there is a suitable ordering of equations and endogenous variables so that a large model can be set out in this way is itself a non-trivial computer exercise, but one worth doing. A block-recursive structure is a feature of most recent large models.

The absence of an explicit reduced form for a non-linear model implies that the multiplier expressions derived earlier no longer apply. Indeed, the multipliers are no longer functions of the structural parameters alone, but in general depend on the values of some of the variables, and so themselves take different values depending on the situation in which they are evaluated. This corresponds to the dependence of elasticities in linear models on the variable values at which they are calculated. As a simple illustration consider the following two-equation national income system:

$$C_t = \beta_1 Y_t + \beta_2 Y_t^2 + u_t$$

$$Y_t = C_t + I_t + G_t.$$

With $\beta_2 < 0$, this gives a declining m.p.c. as income rises. (The consumption function can be estimated by instrumental variables, treating $Y_t^2$ as another endogenous variable). On substituting for $C_t$ in the second equation, and neglecting the error term, the equation corresponding to the reduced form for $Y_t$ in a linear model is

$$\beta_2 Y_t^2 + (\beta_1 - 1)Y_t + (I_t + G_t) = 0,$$

which in general has a pair of solutions. From the solution, or by differentiating this equation, we obtain

$$\frac{\partial Y_t}{\partial I_t} = \frac{1}{1 - \beta_1 - 2\beta_2 Y_t},$$

thus the multiplier depends on the value of $Y_t$ at which it is calculated, and in practice this would be taken to be a "typical" or "current" value. Hence for policy analysis in non-linear models it is necessary to specify the actual values of variables of the model, and multipliers may be different at different states of the economy.

In these situations dynamic multiplier analysis proceeds by simulation methods. Solutions for the endogenous variables over a number of periods are obtained by the methods discussed above, and the effect of a unit change in an exogenous variable is obtained by recomputing the solution with the changed value of that variable. If this exercise is done outside the sample period, with known values of the exogenous variables, then the sequence of ex-post forecasts $\bar{y}_{T+j}$, $j = 1, 2, \ldots$ gives the "control solution" or "base run". Let $y^*_{T+j}$ be the disturbed solution obtained when a particular exogenous variable $x_{k,T+j}$ is replaced by $x_{k,T+j} + \delta, j = 1, 2, \ldots$. The dynamic multipliers are then given as $(y^*_{T+j} - \bar{y}_{T+j})/\delta, j = 1, 2, \ldots$. Thus the multipliers, although obtained in a completely different way, still describe the changes in the endogenous variables over time in response to a unit change in an exogenous variable. Note that if the model is highly non-linear, these multipliers may vary with the size of the perturbation $\delta$; however this does not seem to be a serious problem in practice.

In a linear model, study of the effects of a change in a *parameter* value (that is, a structural change) require more computation than exogenous variable multipliers, since a new reduced form, based on adjusted structural parameters, has to be computed for each change (which explains why Suits (1962) alters the intercept of his tax function rather than the tax rate). In the non-linear case the computational burden is already high since a complete solution path is computed for each change under consideration, and it is in general immaterial whether this is a change in an exogenous variable or a parameter value.

This method is used by Evans (1969a) to calculate estimates of the balanced budget multipliers of the Wharton quarterly econometric forecasting model, as described by Evans and Klein (1968). To give the flavour of the findings, if non-defence government spending is increased by \$1 billion and personal taxes raised by the same amount to give an ex-ante balanced budget, the multiplier is 0.85 in the first quarter declining to 0.31 after 40 quarters. This generates a surplus since the increase in government expenditure itself generates an increase in tax revenues. If an ex-post balanced budget multiplier is required then following a \$1 billion increase in government spending personal taxes must be adjusted each quarter by the amount necessary to balance the budget ex-post. This procedure yields multipliers of 1.72, 2.50, 1.91, \ldots, 1.23 (after 40 quarters). These latter values are higher, as one would expect, since the required increase in personal taxes is less than the \$1 billion imposed in the ex-ante case. Note that since linear methods are no longer appropriate, one would not expect the balanced budget multiplier to be equal to the difference between the expenditure multiplier and the tax multiplier.

Policy analysis proceeds in exactly the same way. Klein (1969) uses the Brookings model to analyse the effect of the 1964 tax cut. A control solution $\bar{y}_{T+k}$ is calculated for the eight quarters 1963-64 using actual tax parameters, whose values changed at the beginning of 1964. A "status quo" solution is also calculated by keeping the tax parameters fixed at their 1963 levels throughout the 1964 calculations. The difference between the two solutions for the various endogenous variables of interest over the four quarters of 1964 then gives an estimate of the effect of the tax cut. Klein estimates that real GNP rose above its no-tax-cut value by \$11.3 billion after four quarters, and that the unemployment rate was reduced by about 0.5 per cent.

Policy simulations with a previous version of the Treasury model are reported by Evans and Riley (1974). They describe the responses of various endogenous variables over a 16-quarter period to an increase in government consumption, an income tax cut, a purchase tax cut, an uprating of National Insurance contributions and benefits, and an increase in world trade. GDP multipliers are calculated not only for policy measures but also for different categories of expenditure. After 16 quarters the (real) GDP multiplier is 1.12 for an income tax cut and 1.33 for an increase in government consumption: in the income tax case there is greater leakage into savings, imports and indirect taxes. Of course, and as a result of these leakages, these values are much lower than the multipliers of simple text-book models, and variations in the import and tax content of different expenditure items also account for variations in the associated GDP multipliers. Finally the Treasury model solution program permits the specification of target values of sets of endogenous variables, and then calculates the required values of given exogenous variables used as policy instruments, equal in number to the number of targets.

### STOCHASTIC SIMULATION

The preceding discussion has tended to ignore the random disturbance terms in behavioural equations, and so has proceeded as if the models were exact. In forecasting exercises this neglect might be justified by arguing that, even when the presence of the disturbance term is acknowledged, in the absence of information about its likely value the best that one can do is to set it equal to its expected value of zero. However the disturbance can be incorporated in studies of the dynamic properties of stochastic models by adding artificially generated random numbers to the estimated equations, and this approach is termed *stochastic simulation*. This is not intended to improve the forecasts, but simply to see whether the behaviour of the endogenous variables as given by the model acknowledging the presence of random variation approximates the behaviour of the actual series. Thus further information about the dynamics of the model and the accuracy of its representation of the real world is obtained.

Adelman and Adelman (1959) investigated the dynamic properties of the 25-equation U.S. annual model of Klein and Goldberger (1955) in this way. (A linearised version of the model was used, to avoid problems discussed in the previous section.) Having added disturbance terms to the estimated structural equations, the solution of the system gives each endogenous variable in terms of predetermined variables and error terms. By assuming that the exogenous variables follow linear trends, and using computer generated random values of the error terms (with variances equal to the sample-period residual variances), values of the endogenous variables are obtained. The Adelmans found that the generated paths of the endogenous variables exhibited cyclical fluctuations about linear trends. Their answer to the question of how to assess the correspondence between the behaviour of the simulated values and the actual series was to apply the National Bureau of Economic Research business cycle methodology to the simulated series. In terms of the length of cycles, the coincidence of turning points of various series, and the lead-lag relationship of various series to the reference cycle, the simulated fluctuations were "remarkably similar to those described by the NBER as characterising the United States economy". Thus they concluded that the Klein-Goldberger model, with the presence of random errors acknowledged, provided a useful approximation to the U.S. economy. Studies contained in Hickman (1972) report similar findings for more recent large U.S. quarterly models, with one important modification. To improve the cyclical correspondence between the actual and simulated series, it is necessary to ensure that the artificial disturbance terms are cross-correlated and autocorrelated to the same extent as the sample-period residuals.

These random errors in the equations were the Adelmans' "shocks of Type II", and they also investigated the effect of "shocks of Type I", namely random errors added to the linear projections of the exogenous variables so that these behaved more like observed series. In practice there was little improvement in realism using shocks of Type I, for the predicted endogenous variables still had very smooth trends, without the sort of cyclical behaviour observed in the actual economy.

In some situations it may be important to remember that in non-linear models the mean of a set of stochastic simulations is not necessarily equal to the non-stochastic solution. Clearly in a linear model there is no problem: a set of solution paths generated by using different realisations for the random errors and for each realisation solving

$$\hat{B}y^{\dagger}_{T+j} + \hat{\Gamma}z_{T+j} = u_{T+j}, \quad j = 1,2,\ldots$$

will have a mean given by (apart from sampling fluctuations) the solution path obtained by solving

$$\hat{B}\tilde{y}_{T+j} + \hat{\Gamma}z_{T+j} = 0.$$

However in the non-linear case the mean of the solutions obtained from

$$f_i(y^{\dagger}_{T+j}, z_{T+j}, \hat{\theta}_i) = u_{i,T+j}, \quad i=1,\ldots,G, \quad j=1,2,\ldots$$

for a sample of realisations of the error process is not given by the solution of

$$f_i(\tilde{y}_{T+j}, z_{T+j}, \hat{\theta}_i) = 0, \quad i=1,\ldots,G, \quad j=1,2,\ldots$$

thus forecasts based on this last equation are not in general unbiased. A simple illustration is given by the relation

$$y = Ax^{\beta}e^{u}$$

which would be estimated as the log-linear regression

$$\log y = \log A + \beta \log x + u.$$

In the present notation the function $f$ is given as $\log y - \log A - \beta \log x$, and equating this to zero and solving for $y$ given $x$ yields the forecast

$$\tilde{y} = Ax^\beta .$$

However if $u$ is normally distributed with mean 0 and variance $\sigma^2$, so that $\exp(u)$ is log-normally distributed, then $y$ has expected value

$$E(y) = Ax^\beta e^{\frac{1}{2}\sigma^2} .$$

Thus the forecast error $y - \tilde{y}$ does not have a zero mean, even in this example where the parameters have been assumed known.

### FORECAST COMPARISONS

A common device for evaluating the performance of an empirical macroeconometric model has been a comparison of its forecasting performance against that of some simpler forecasting rules. In the words of Cooper (1972, pp.828-9): "Comparing an econometric to a naïve method of forecasting supplies a technique for assessing the economic information contained in an econometric model. The defining characteristic of a 'naïve' forecasting method is that it depends exclusively on purely statistical properties of economic time series, such as trend, past levels, or past changes. A naïve method does not incorporate any economic information ... Forecasts made by naïve methods are then compared with forecasts made by other methods. Forecasting methods that cannot do better than a purely mechanical one should be discarded." Over the years the forecasting methods against which econometric models have been compared have gradually become less naïve, which is a mild acknowledgement of progress! Initially "no-change" ($\hat{y}_{T+1} = y_T$) or "same-change" ($\hat{y}_{T+1} - y_T = y_T - y_{T-1}$) forecasting rules were employed. Subsequently autoregressive models of the form

$$y_t = \phi_1 y_{t-1} + \phi_2 y_{t-2} + \ldots + \phi_p y_{t-p} + \epsilon_t$$

fitted to the relevant series one-at-a-time have been used to generate forecasts, as have autoregressive-moving average (ARMA) models

$$y_t - \phi_1 y_{t-1} - \cdots - \phi_p y_{t-p} = \epsilon_t - \theta_1 \epsilon_{t-1} - \cdots - \theta_q \epsilon_{t-q}.$$

Nelson (1972) compares the FRB-MIT-PENN model against ARMA models for certain key endogenous variables, and while in sample-period comparisons the econometric model was ahead, once the comparison moved outside the sample, the "pure time-series" models had smaller forecast errors.

Cooper's (1972) study is more extensive, and has generated more debate. Cooper took seven quarterly U.S. models, and in an attempt to ensure comparability re-estimated them, by the same procedure, for the same data period (even though this was not necessarily the same period used by the model-builders), then carried out within-sample and post-sample (ex-post) comparisons, across models and with purely autoregressive models. In summary, the autoregressive models generally had smaller forecast errors than the econometric models, although this result has not gone unchallenged. First, Cooper's comparisons are confined to one-period forecasts, and there is a tendency for the prediction intervals of autoregressive models to widen more rapidly. More generally, Howrey *et al.* (1974) raise objections to the mechanical fitting of a model, especially to a body of data different from that originally employed and having in mind the model-builder's application of what is touchingly called "tender loving care", and question the relevance of the findings to genuine ex-ante forecasting. In practical prediction exercises, good information about exogenous shifts and structural breaks is often available – changes in legislation, institutional arrangements, labour contracts and so forth are often known in advance – so the forecaster will amend the model to take these into account. In practice this is frequently accomplished by adjusting the constant term in estimated equations, and although this is equivalent to assigning a non-zero residual to the equation, the alternative explanation in terms of autocorrelated residuals is typically less preferred, since these eventually tend back to zero whereas the shifts under consideration are usually thought to be persistent.

The idea that "purely statistical" models for endogenous variables provide independent checks on the econometric model can also be challenged. In general, if the exogenous variables of the model have time series representations of the autoregressive or ARMA form, then the econometric model implies the existence of a similar representation for the endogenous variables, which thus cannot be used as an *independent* check on the forecasting performance of the model (Prothero and Wallis, 1976; Wallis, 1977; Zellner and Palm, 1974). To illustrate, we consider a simple dynamic model used in chapter I, namely

$$C_t = \beta Y_t + \gamma C_{t-1} + u_t$$

$$Y_t = C_t + I_t$$

and now assume that the exogenous variable is generated by

$$I_t = \rho I_{t-1} + \epsilon_t,$$

where $\epsilon$ and $u$ are independent (to ensure the exogeneity of $I$). To obtain the time series model for $Y$, we first write these three equations together, using the matrix lag operator notation introduced above:

$$\begin{bmatrix} 1-\gamma L & -\beta & 0 \\ -1 & 1 & -1 \\ 0 & 0 & 1-\rho L \end{bmatrix} \begin{bmatrix} C_t \\ Y_t \\ I_t \end{bmatrix} = \begin{bmatrix} u_t \\ 0 \\ \epsilon_t \end{bmatrix}.$$

The determinant of the matrix is $(1-\rho L)(1-\gamma L-\beta)$, and on taking the adjoint matrix to the right-hand side, the "final equation" for $Y_t$ in this system is obtained as

$$(1-\rho L)(1-\gamma L-\beta)Y_t = (1-\rho L)u_t + (1-\gamma L)\epsilon_t$$

$$= u_t - \rho u_{t-1} + \epsilon_t - \gamma \epsilon_{t-1}.$$

The polynomial on the left-hand side is of second degree, and the right-hand side is the sum of two moving averages of independent variables, which by a result in time series theory is equivalent to a moving average of the same order in a single random error, $\eta_t$ say. The net effect is that, by virtue of the assumptions made, there exists an ARMA model for $Y_t$ of the form

$$Y_t - \phi_1 Y_{t-1} - \phi_2 Y_{t-2} = \eta_t - \theta_1 \eta_{t-1}.$$

Thus a "statistical" forecasting relationship is implied by the underlying dynamic model: it is an alternative solution form, and so cannot provide a separate, independent set of forecasts for comparative purposes. In general a correctly specified econometric model, with its explicit representation of the various interrelationships and restrictions, would be expected to outperform the statistical forecasting relations. In this example, ex-ante one-period forecasts of income are obtained from the reduced form as

$$\hat{Y}_{T+1} = \frac{1}{1-\beta}(\gamma C_T + \hat{I}_{T+1}),$$

with the forecast $\hat{I}_{T+1}$ being calculated from the model for this variable as $\rho I_T$. It can be shown that the error variance of these model-based forecasts is no greater than, and generally less than, the error variance of forecasts based on the pure time-series model for $Y_t$.

One might then ask, why do the practical comparisons often produce the opposite conclusion to this theoretical result? Noting that the result is based on a linear model with known parameters, clearly non-linearities and parameter estimation errors may have a different impact on the two approaches to forecasting. More generally, however, the model is assumed to be correct and in practice one doubts this assumption insofar as the dynamic and stochastic specification of large models is concerned. In these areas there is little guidance from economic theory, and one suspects that, taking a large model equation-by-equation, relatively less systematic attention is given to these matters than when a time series model is identified for a single endogenous variable. We have argued that these forecast comparisons do not provide an independent check on the performance of a model, but they can be seen as a model specification check, since in the light of the foregoing results a smaller forecast error variance for the "naïve" time series model indicates that at least the dynamic and stochastic specification of the model is not correct. Many of the models in Hickman (1972) used by Cooper exhibit substantial residual autocorrelation which, as noted above, needs to be incorporated in stochastic simulations to ensure realistic solution paths. Since the time series relations emphasise precisely this aspect of the behaviour of the variables, Cooper's results are less surprising. Rather than providing an independent final check, comparisons with time series models are an aid to model-building, and when the comparisons turn out as in these studies the conclusion is that the econometrician's task is not over.

# REFERENCES

Adelman, I. and Adelman, F. L. (1959). The dynamic properties of the Klein-Goldberger model. *Econometrica*, 27, 597-625. Reprinted in Gordon and Klein (1966), Hooper and Nerlove (1970), and Zellner (1968).

Aigner, D., Lovell, C. A. K. and Schmidt, P. (1977). Formulation and estimation of stochastic frontier production function models. *Journal of Econometrics*, 6, 21-37.

Allen, R. G. D. (1938). *Mathematical Analysis for Economists*. London: Macmillan.

Almon, S. (1965). The distributed lag between capital appropriations and expenditures. *Econometrica*, 33, 178-196. Reprinted in Zellner (1968).

Arrow, K. J., Chenery, H. B., Minhas, B. S. and Solow, R. M. (1961). Capital-labor substitution and economic efficiency. *Review of Economics and Statistics*, 43, 225-250. Reprinted in Zellner (1968).

Attfield, C. L. F. (1976). Estimation of the structural parameters in a permanent income model. *Economica*, 43, 247-254.

Ball, R. J. and Drake, P. S. (1964). The relationship between aggregate consumption and wealth. *International Economic Review*, 5, 63-81.

Barker, T. S. (ed.) (1976). *Economic Structure and Policy*. London: Chapman and Hall.

Berndt, E. R. and Christensen, L. R. (1973). The translog function and the substitution of equipment, structures and labor in U.S. manufacturing 1929-68. *Journal of Econometrics*, 1, 81-113.

Bischoff, C. W. (1969). Hypothesis testing and the demand for capital goods. *Review of Economics and Statistics*, 51, 354-368.

Brechling, F. (1975). *Investment and Employment Decisions*. Manchester: University Press.

Brown, M. and De Cani, J. S. (1963). Technological change and the distribution of income. *International Economic Review*, 4, 289-309.

Brown, T. M. (1952). Habit persistence and lags in consumer behaviour. *Econometrica*, 20, 355-371. Reprinted in Hooper and Nerlove (1970).

Cagan, P. (1958). Monetary dynamics of hyperinflation. In *Studies in the Quantity Theory of Money* (ed. M. Friedman), pp.25-117. Chicago: University Press.

Christ, C. F. *et al.* (1963). *Measurement in Economics*. Stanford: University Press.

Christensen, L. R., Jorgenson, D. W. and Lau, L. J. (1973). Transcendental logarithmic production frontiers. *Review of Economics and Statistics*, 55, 28-45.

Cobb, C. W. and Douglas, P. H. (1928). A theory of production. *American Economic Review*, 18, (supplement), 139-165.

Committee on Policy Optimisation (R. J. Ball, Chairman) (1978). *Report* (Cmnd. 7148). London: HMSO.

Cooper, R. L. (1972). The predictive performance of quarterly econometric models of the United States. In Hickman (1972), pp.813-926.

Cramer, J. S. (1969). *Empirical Econometrics*. Amsterdam: North-Holland.

Davidson, J. E. H., Hendry, D. F., Srba, F. and Yeo, S. (1978). Econometric modelling of the aggregate time-series relationship between consumers' expenditure and income in the United Kingdom. *Economic Journal*, 88, 661-692.

Davis, T. E. (1952). The consumption function as a tool for prediction. *Review of Economics and Statistics*, 34, 270-277.

Deaton, A. (1977). Involuntary saving through unanticipated inflation. *American Economic Review*, 67, 899-910.

De Leeuw, F. (1962). The demand for capital goods by manufacturers: a study of quarterly time series. *Econometrica*, 30, 407-423.

Douglas, P. H. (1948). Are there laws of production? *American Economic Review*, 38, 1-41.

Duesenberry, J. S. (1949). *Income, Saving, and the Theory of Consumer Behavior*. Cambridge, Mass.: Harvard University Press.

Duesenberry, J. S., Fromm, G., Klein, L. R. and Kuh, E. (eds.) (1965). *The Brookings Quarterly Econometric Model of the U.S. Economy*. Chicago: Rand-McNally.

——————— (1969). *The Brookings Model: Some Further Results*. Chicago: Rand-McNally.

Eisner, R. and Nadiri, M. I. (1968). Investment behavior and neo-classical theory. *Review of Economics and Statistics*, 50, 369-382.

——————— (1970). Neoclassical theory of investment behavior: a comment. *Review of Economics and Statistics*, 52, 216-222.

Eisner, R. and Strotz, R. H. (1963). Determinants of business investment. In *Impacts of Monetary Policy* (Commission on Money and Credit), pp.60-138. Englewood Cliffs, N.J.: Prentice-Hall.

Evans, H. P. and Riley, C. J. (1974). *Simulations with the Treasury Model*. (Government Economic Service Occasional Paper No.8). London: HMSO.

Evans, M. K. (1967). A study of industry investment decisions. *Review of Economics and Statistics*, 49, 151-164.

——————— (1969). *Macroeconomic Activity*. New York: Harper and Row.

——————— (1969a). Reconstruction and estimation of the balanced budget multiplier. *Review of Economics and Statistics*, 51, 14-25.

Evans, M. K. and Klein, L. R. (1968). *The Wharton Econometric Forecasting Model*. Philadelphia: University of Pennsylvania Press.

Farrell, M. J. (1957). The measurement of productive efficiency. *Journal of the Royal Statistical Society*, A, 120, 253-281.

Friedman, M. (1957). *A Theory of the Consumption Function*. Princeton, N.J.: University Press for National Bureau of Economic Research.

Fromm, G. and Klein, L. R. (eds.) (1975). *The Brookings Model: Perspective and Recent Developments*. Amsterdam: North-Holland.

——————— (1976). The NBER/NSF model comparison seminar: an analysis of results. *Annals of Economic and Social Measurement*, 5, 1-28.

Fuchs, V. R. (1963). Capital-labor substitution: a note. *Review of Economics and Statistics*, 45, 436-438.

Glaister, S. (1978). *Mathematical Methods for Economists* (2nd ed.). Oxford: Basil Blackwell.

Goldberger, A. S. (1959). *Impact Multipliers and Dynamic Properties of the Klein-Goldberger Model*. Amsterdam: North-Holland.

Goldsmith, R. W. (1955). *A Study of Saving in the United States, I*. Princeton, N.J.: University Press.

Gordon, R. A. and Klein, L. R. (eds.) (1966). *Readings in Business Cycles.* London: Allen and Unwin.

Gould, J. P. (1969). The use of endogenous variables in dynamic models of investment. *Quarterly Journal of Economics,* 83, 580-599.

Griliches, Z. and Ringstad, V. (1971). *Economies of Scale and the Form of the Production Function.* Amsterdam: North-Holland.

Haavelmo, T. (1947). Methods of measuring the marginal propensity to consume. *Journal of the American Statistical Association,* 42, 105-122. Reprinted in Hood, W. C. and Koopmans, T. C. (eds.) (1953), *Studies in Econometric Method.* New York: Wiley.

Harberger, A. C. (ed.) (1960). *The Demand for Durable Goods.* Chicago: University Press.

Hickman, B. G. (ed.) (1972). *Econometric Models of Cyclical Behavior.* New York: Columbia University Press. (NBER Studies in Income and Wealth, No.36).

Hines, A. G. (1964). Trade unions and wage inflation in the United Kingdom, 1893-1961. *Review of Economic Studies,* 31, 221-252.

Hogan, W. P. (1958). Technical progress and production functions. *Review of Economics and Statistics,* 40, 407-411.

Hooper, J. W. and Nerlove, M. (eds.) (1970). *Selected Readings in Econometrics from Econometrica.* London: M.I.T. Press.

Howrey, E. P., Klein, L. R. and McCarthy, M. D. (1974). Notes on testing the predictive performance of econometric models. *International Economic Review,* 15, 366-383.

Johansen, L. (1959). Substitution versus fixed production coefficients in the theory of economic growth: a synthesis. *Econometrica,* 27, 157-176.

——————— (1972). *Production Functions.* Amsterdam: North-Holland.

Jorgenson, D. W. (1963). Capital theory and investment behavior. *American Economic Review,* 53, 247-259. Reprinted in Gordon and Klein (1966).

——————— (1965). Anticipations and investment behavior. In Duesenberry *et al.* (1965), pp.35-92.

——————— (1967). The theory of investment behavior. In *Determinants of Investment Behavior* (ed. R. Ferber), pp.129-155. New York: National Bureau of Economic Research.

——————— (1971). Econometric studies of investment behavior: a survey. *Journal of Economic Literature,* 9, 1111-1147.

Jorgenson, D. W. and Stephenson, J. S. (1967a). Investment behavior in U.S. manufacturing, 1947-1960. *Econometrica,* 35, 169-220.

——————— (1967b). The time structure of investment behavior in United States manufacturing, 1947-1960. *Review of Economics and Statistics,* 49, 16-27.

——————— (1969a). Anticipations and investment behavior in U.S. manufacturing, 1947-1960. *Journal of the American Statistical Association,* 64, 67-89.

——————— (1969b). Issues in the development of the neoclassical theory of investment behavior. *Review of Economics and Statistics,* 51, 346-353.

Keynes, J. M. (1936). *The General Theory of Employment, Interest and Money.* London: Macmillan.

Klein, L. R. (1950). *Economic Fluctuations in the United States, 1921-1941.* Cowles Commission Monograph 11. New York: Wiley.

———————— (1953). *A Textbook of Econometrics*. Evanston, Ill.: Row, Peterson.

———————— (1969). Econometric analysis of the tax cut of 1964. In Duesenberry *et al.* (1969), pp.459-472.

———————— (1974). Issues in econometric studies of investment behavior. *Journal of Economic Literature*, 12, 43-49.

Klein, L. R., Ball, R. J., Hazelwood, A. and Vandome, P. (1961). *An Econometric Model of the United Kingdom*. Oxford: University Press.

Klein, L. R. and Goldberger, A. S. (1955). *An Econometric Model of the United States, 1929-1952*. Amsterdam: North-Holland.

Kmenta, J. (1967). On estimation of the CES production function. *International Economic Review*, 8, 180-189.

Koyck, L. M. (1954) *Distributed Lags and Investment Analysis*. Amsterdam: North-Holland.

Kuznets, S. (1942). *Uses of National Income in Peace and War*. National Bureau of Economic Research, Occasional Paper No.6.

Laury, J. S. E., Lewis, G. R. and Ormerod, P. A. (1978). Properties of macroeconomic models of the U.K. economy: a comparative study. *National Institute Economic Review*, No.83, 52-72.

L'Esperance, W. L. (1964). A case study in prediction: the market for watermelons. *Econometrica*, 32, 163-173.

Liviatan, N. (1963). Tests of the permanent income hypothesis based on a re-interview savings survey. In Christ (1963), pp.29-59. Reprinted in Zellner (1968).

Mizon, G. E. (1977). Inferential procedures in nonlinear models: an application in a UK industrial cross section study of factor substitution and returns to scale. *Econometrica*, 45, 1221-1242.

Modigliani, F. and Ando, A. K. (1957). Tests of the life cycle hypothesis of savings. *Bulletin of the Oxford University Institute of Statistics*, 19, 99-124.

Mueller, M. G. (ed.) (1969). *Readings in Macroeconomics*. London: Holt, Rinehart and Winston.

Nadiri, M. I. and Rosen, S. (1969). Interrelated factor demand functions. *American Economic Review*, 59, 457-471.

———————— (1973). *A Disequilibrium Model of Demand for Factors of Production*. New York: National Bureau of Economic Research.

Nelson, C. R. (1972). The prediction performance of the FRB-MIT-PENN model of the U.S. economy. *American Economic Review*, 62, 902-917.

Nerlove, M. (1960). The market demand for durable goods: a comment. *Econometrica*, 28, 132-142.

———————— (1963). Returns to scale in electricity supply. In Christ (1963), pp.167-198. Reprinted in Zellner (1968).

———————— (1966). A tabular survey of macroeconometric models. *International Economic Review*, 7, 127-175.

———————— (1967). Recent empirical studies of the CES and related production functions. In *The Theory and Empirical Analysis of Production* (Studies in Income and Wealth Volume 31), pp.55-122. New York: National Bureau of Economic Research.

Nickell, S. J. (1978). *The Investment Decisions of Firms*. Cambridge: University Press.

Posner, M. V. (ed.) (1978). *Demand Management*. London: Heinemann Educational Books.

Prothero, D. L. and Wallis, K. F. (1976). Modelling macroeconomic time series (with discussion). *Journal of the Royal Statistical Society*, A, 139, 468-500.

Renton, G. A. (ed.) (1975). *Modelling the Economy.* London: Heinemann Educational Books.

Samuelson, P. A. (1939). Interactions between the multiplier analysis and the principle of acceleration. *Review of Economics and Statistics*, 21, 75-78. Reprinted in Mueller (1969).

Sargan, J. D. (1971). Production functions: theoretical considerations. In *Qualified Manpower and Economic Performance* (P. R. G. Layard, J. D. Sargan, M. E. Ager and D. J. Jones), pp.149-166. London: Allen Lane.

Schmidt, P. (1976). On the statistical estimation of parametric frontier production functions. *Review of Economics and Statistics*, 58, 238-239.

Solow, R. M. (1957). Technical change and the aggregate production function. *Review of Economics and Statistics*, 39, 312-320. Reprinted in Mueller (1969) and Zellner (1968).

Stone, R. and Rowe, D. A. (1960). The durability of consumer's durable goods. *Econometrica*, 28, 407-416. Reprinted in Hooper and Nerlove (1970) and Zellner (1968).

Suits, D. B. (1955). An econometric model of the watermelon market. *Journal of Farm Economics*, 37, 237-251.

————— (1962). Forecasting and analysis with an econometric model. *American Economic Review*, 52, 104-132. Reprinted in Gordon and Klein (1966) and Zellner (1968).

Theil, H. and Boot, J. C. G. (1962). The final form of econometric equation systems. *Review of the International Statistical Institute*, 30, 136-152. Reprinted in Zellner (1968).

Thomas, R. L. and Stoney, P. J. M. (1970). A note on the dynamic properties of the Hines inflation model. *Review of Economic Studies*, 37, 286-294.

Tinbergen, J. (1939). *Statistical Testing of Business-Cycle Theories, II: Business Cycles in the U.S.A., 1919-1932.* Geneva: League of Nations.

————— (1951). *Business Cycles in the United Kingdom, 1870-1914.* Amsterdam: North-Holland.

Tobin, J. (1967). Comment (on Jorgenson, 1967). In *Determinants of Investment Behavior* (ed. R. Ferber), pp.156-160. New York: National Bureau of Economic Research.

Townend, J. C. (1976). The personal saving ratio. *Bank of England Quarterly Bulletin*, 16, 53-73.

Tyrni, I. (1964). The effect of price changes on consumer saving. *Review of Economic Studies*, 31, 149-162.

Wallis, K. F. (1972). *Introductory Econometrics.* Oxford: Basil Blackwell.

————— (1977). Multiple time series analysis and the final form of econometric models. *Econometrica*, 45, 1481-1497.

Wold, H. O. A. (1958). A case study of interdependent versus causal chain systems. *Review of the International Statistical Institute*, 26, 5-25.

Worswick, G. D. N. and Blackaby, F. T. (eds.) (1974). *The Medium-Term: Models of the British Economy.* London: Heinemann Educational Books.

Zellner, A. (ed.) (1968). *Readings in Economic Statistics and Econometrics.* Boston: Little, Brown.

Zellner, A. and Palm, F. (1974). Time series analysis and simultaneous equation econometric models. *Journal of Econometrics*, 2, 17-54.

# INDEX OF NAMES